Words of This Life
Occasional Reflections on the Spiritual Life

by
Fr. Richard Rene

To my wife Jaime and my children
Lily, Gabriel and John
and
The citizens of Cranbrook, British Columbia
who kept up their subscriptions

Contents

Foreword

The book that follows is a collection of articles published in the *Cranbrook Daily Townsman* from spring 2008 until the present. Together they represent an engagement between myself, an Eastern Orthodox Christian priest, and the people of Cranbrook, British Columbia. On a more general level, though, these articles are one instance of a wider, ongoing conversation between the ancient tradition of Eastern Orthodox Christianity and a contemporary world steeped in the western sensibility of social, cultural and religious pluralism, materialism and secularism.

Through the exploration of a wide variety of topics—from Church history to blockbuster movies—my work attempts to kindle in my readers a sense of the profound and wide-ranging ramifications of the Christian Gospel, which is simply the entrance of God into history and the reunion of creation with its Creator in the Incarnation of Jesus Christ of Nazareth. If I were to lift up one message from these diverse reflections, it would simply be "God is with us." God's full self-revelation in Jesus Christ means that every aspect of human life, from the mundane to the lofty, contains within itself the spark of divine life. And, once the dust and ashes that covers much of our fallen existence is blown away, that spark can flare up into a flame to light up the whole world with God's glory. These articles are attempts to blow on the embers.

Throughout my work, I have proceeded with certain assumptions, which may be worth noting. First, I hold beyond question the absolute truth of the Gospel of Jesus as it prophesied in the Old Testament scriptures, testified to in the four Gospels and the New Testament, and understood and taught by the Apostles and their spiritual descendents from the beginning. This scriptural Gospel has been preserved continuously and uninterruptedly for two thousand years in the writings of the Church Fathers, the formulae of the creeds, the decisions of councils, the canons that apply the faith to specific circumstances, the art and architecture of

Church buildings, and the lives of holy men and women through the ages. It is a faith that continues to be held today—in all of its fullness—in the life and worship of the Eastern Orthodox Church.

Second, the Gospel that I hold and teach leads me to the conviction that the world around me, though fallen, remains "good," as God made it and declared it to be from the beginning. If the man Jesus Christ is indeed the eternal Word of God, then the world itself is created in the image and likeness of Jesus Christ. To paraphrase someone, creation was made in the shape of the Cross. As such, the world that I encounter as a Christian cannot be seen as totally depraved and utterly degenerate, awaiting my words to bring light into utter darkness. Rather, I see the Gospel and the truth as *latent* in the world, awaiting a name rather than an existence. As the Apostle Paul said to the men of Athens, "What therefore you worship as unknown, I proclaim to you." (Acts 17:23) My assumption is that God is not far from each one of us. As a priest and a writer on matters theological, my role is that of a midwife, assisting to deliver a life that was planted in us by Word who created us, and therefore already exists within us, waiting to be born.

Given these two basic presuppositions, my writings at once affirm the absolute belief in Jesus Christ as He has been revealed, proclaimed, and taught in the Eastern Orthodox Church, while simultaneously affirming the good in all areas of life, upholding what I believe to be of absolute worth, not only in other Christian communities, but in every form of spiritual and secular life that our complex world has to offer. On the one hand, my insistence on engaging affirmatively with these "outsiders" may offend purists, both within the Orthodox Church and among some of my Protestant or Roman Catholic brethren. On the other hand, my insistence on the absolute rightness of the Christian Gospel as it is articulated in the life of the Eastern Orthodox Church may well upset those who incline toward spiritual pluralism and relativism.

To either group I make no apology and offer no defence.

Here is where I stand.

For the ease and convenience of the reader, I have divided the articles following into seven sections. These are not subject headings in any exhaustive sense. There is no systematic line of reasoning here. In their original form, the articles were occasional pieces written to meet a deadline. In compiling this book, I simply tried to find commonalities in audience and general subject matter. While some articles follow an order—usually demanded by the subject itself—the sections are presented more or less randomly.

A Gospel for All represents pieces aimed at those who call themselves "Christian" in some sense. It addresses areas of ethics, worship, and the spiritual life that tend to be specific to those who grapple with Christian faith.

A Taste of the Fullness addresses Christian issues from the standpoint of Eastern Orthodoxy. The goal here was to introduce non-Orthodox Christians to an understanding they may not have encountered.

Baptizing the Culture is a sampling of my attempts to engage as an Orthodox Christian with secular culture in its various forms. The majority of the articles deal with spiritual themes in movies and television, but the section contains one major essay responding the phenomenon of violence in contemporary life.

Keyholes into Church History are precisely that: reflective glimpses into key events in the history of Christianity. Taken together, they may form a rudimentary introduction to Church history—a kind "idiot's guide to the idiot's guide," though I offer suggested resources by which the readers may expand their understanding.

Sanctification of Time offers a few fruits from articles I wrote when my deadline fell close to a specific feast day celebration in the Orthodox Church. The articles included do not cover all the feast days (that alone would require a library of books, let alone one book), but they do offer a sampling of the ways in which the Eastern Orthodox calendar infuses the Gospel into our daily, weekly and yearly experience of temporal reality.

Signposts on the Daily Walk is the largest section, aimed at the newspaper's largely non-Christian audience. My goal in writing these pieces was to somehow offer spiritual nourishment and guidance—without preaching or laying out platitudes—to a pluralistic audience. Again, my assumption is that nurturing of goodness in any life is ultimately a proclamation of God's own goodness.

Finally, **To the Unknown God** specifically aims to direct those who would call themselves "spiritual seekers"—those who feel a certain dissatisfaction with the *status quo* of their secular lives, and want to grow in spiritual directions, but are not certain how to do so. As in previous articles, my approach has been to try to offer direction without enforcing the destination.

In the writing of this book, I would like to thank my beloved wife Jaime, for her patience in reading and critiquing the work of this frequently overly-sensitive writer; my children Lily, Gabriel and John, for allowing Daddy to work in peace; the members of Saint Aidan's Orthodox Church, for supporting their priest in doing the work of an evangelist; Barry Coulter, the editor of the *Cranbrook Daily Townsman*, for providing me this precious outlet to the world; and finally, the subscribers and citizens of Cranbrook, for keeping an open mind, even when they disagreed. Such are the joys of our community, which in the end, is called to be nothing less than an image of that eternally joyful and loving divine community—the Holy Trinity—of which we can all claim a part as children and heirs of God through Jesus Christ.

May 2011

A Gospel for All

Authority is Not a Four Letter Word

Authority. Just mentioning the word in the context of religion conjures up images of manipulative TV evangelists, dictatorial Imams, and abusive priests.

Our instinctive allergy to religious authority may often be justified. Too often has religion become a means for charismatic individuals to satisfy their own lust for power, at the expense of their flocks. We do well to stay away from such corruption.

But although many Christian communities endorse oppression and tyranny through a framework of religious legalism, this is not the authentic Christian understanding of how authority works. For one thing, Christianity properly understood is not the daily performance of a set of propositions, legal tenets or rituals to appease a potentially vengeful God. Rather, Christianity is a loving encounter between us and God, in and through the man Jesus — born, crucified and raised from the dead.

The Christian understanding of authority flows directly from the Incarnation. God is indeed all-powerful and just, but His authority is not demonstrated in decrees, punishments and blessings from "on high." Rather, He demonstrated His authority once and for all by emptying Himself in love, to submit to and serve His creation, even to the point of dying with it. In descending those depths of powerlessness on the Cross, He revealed the heights of everything he gave up to do so — all His power and glory as God.

As Saint Paul tells the Philippians, "[He] did not count equality with God a thing to be grasped, but emptied himself, taking the form of a servant, being born in the likeness of men. And being found in human form he humbled himself and became obedient unto death, even death on a cross." (Phil. 2:6-8)

Jesus' self-emptying demonstrates the depths of God's love for the world. At the same time, His identity as the Almighty God crucified in the flesh invests all human suffering and death with a profound depth and meaning that it did not possess before.

Permit me a little analogy here. Imagine Steven Harper arrived in Cranbrook one morning, took off his suit, threw on some overalls, and joined one of our waste disposal crews collecting garbage in the alleys. Assuming this was not some political photo op, this would be an incredible turn of events, don't you think? Harper's spontaneous act of service would demonstrate the best qualities for a leader of our nation.

At the same time, the startling fact of seeing a *Prime Minister* collecting garbage would also serve to highlight the quality and value of what our waste disposal crews do anonymously every week. The service gives value to the authority, and the authority ennobles the service.

Authority, then, is an essential part of what makes loving service to others real. All of us, Christian or not, have to deal with authority by virtue of being parents, older siblings, employers, managers, team leaders, or just adults. Whatever our issues may be with abuses of power inflicted upon us or the world around us, our challenge is not to reject the authority we possess, but to give meaning to it by serving and loving those for whom we are responsible, putting their needs before our own. To borrow the title of one Christian leader, we are to be "the servant of the servants of God."

Without our loving service to others, our authority over them is mere egotism and tyranny. But without our authority, the meaning of service itself is lost and along with it, the meaning of love itself.

June, 2010

Has God got a plan for your life?

Every weekday, I put out a sign that says, "Church Open. Come in and Pray." While the crowds have yet to respond *en masse* to my invitation (and believe me, I'm not holding my breath), it has occasionally borne good fruit.

For instance, just two days ago, I brought in the sign at five o'clock, only to discover someone praying in the Church (gasp!). I indicated that I had no intention of bothering him, and that he could stay as long as he wanted. He, however, wished to talk, and so we sat for a while and shot the spiritual breeze.

At the heart of our conversation was a question so common that I thought it worth addressing in this context: "I know that God is in my life, but I don't know what He wants me to do. What is His plan for me?"

To my mind, the question itself is problematic. Too often we think of God as an omnipresent, omnipotent power that floats above history, orchestrating events according to some divine blueprint, with every eventuality mapped out and anticipated.

We poor humans have little knowledge of God's secret blueprint. We can only muddle along, trying to get an inside track on the portion of God's plan that applies to us. When something unexpected or inexplicable happens, we try to console ourselves that it must have some meaning that we are too inferior to see.

In fact, such an attitude has less to do with the Christian understanding of God, and more to do with Deism — a belief that God is the Supreme Architect who exists at arm's length from earthly concerns. In the Christian view, God is certainly transcendent, all-knowing, all-powerful, everywhere present, etc. But God does not make Himself known to us in these abstract and ultimately non-human terms. Rather, the indescribable, infinite, transcendent God has fully revealed Himself in the person of Jesus Christ.

As I indicated in a previous article, the essence of Jesus'

preaching is "Repent, for the kingdom of God is at hand" (Mark 1:15 and Matt. 4:17), which is to say that the historical man Jesus is the full, complete and final revelation of God's will, wisdom, word, power, and authority in this world. Everything there is to be known of God's will for our lives is completely accessible and knowable in our personal encounter with the Son of God. "For [God] has made known to us in all wisdom and insight the mystery of His will, according to his purpose *which he set forth in Christ as a plan for the fulness of time, to unite all things in him, things in heaven and things on earth.*" (Eph. 1:9-10, emphasis mine)

As I have also said before, this encounter takes place not in the future or the past, but in whatever lies before us at any given moment. This is because human existence is by definition a present existence. Although our minds may dwell in the future or the past, we don't *actually* live then. As human beings, we actually live now and as *a* human being, now is where God revealed Himself to us. As Saint Paul tells his Corinthian hearers, "Now is the acceptable time; behold, now is the day of salvation." (2 Cor. 6:2)

So what is God's plan for *your* life? If by 'plan' you mean some secret blueprint of future events that will lead to a glorious personal destiny, then there isn't one. In another sense, however, God's plan is evident in is whatever situations, tasks and people are in front of you right now. After all, those present realities are where Christ is, and Christ is the final revelation of God's will to us and the world.

John Lennon once sang, "Life is what happens when you're busy making other plans." Amen to that. As long as we continue fumbling around for God's secret blueprint, we will miss out on His will, which is right in front of our noses: love our family and our neighbours, do the day's work as best as we can, play with joy when it's time to play, make the today's decisions conscientiously and with all due diligence; and consciously discover the Presence of God in all these activities by rooting and surrounding them in prayer and worship.

15

Living this way, in time we reflect back on our lives and see patterns and discover meanings. We start to understand why things happened as they did. We witness the guiding hand of Providence in our lives. Such backward reflection, however, is not an end in itself, but a reminder for us to be faithful to Christ *now*, by attending to the demands of His Kingdom, which is always found in whatever is 'at hand.'

"Is it really that simple?" my recent church visitor asked me. Yes, I told him, it really is, and our only challenge is to accept that simplicity. To that end, I offer you the following prayer by Saint Philaret of Moscow: "O Lord, grant that I may greet the coming day in peace. Help me to rely upon Your holy will in every moment. In every hour of every day, reveal Your will to me. Bless my association with those who surround me. Teach me to treat all that comes to me with peace of soul and the firm conviction that Your will governs all. In all my deeds and words, guide my thoughts and feelings. In unforeseen events, let me not forget that all is sent by You. Teach me to act firmly and wisely, without embittering or embarrassing others. Grant me to bear the fatigue of the coming day with all that it shall bring. Direct my will. Teach me to pray, and pray Yourself within me. Amen."

March, 2009

Marriage: Investment, Covenant or Sacrament?

Consider the following situation: you are shopping at the grocery store when you notice a young couple in the aisle ahead of you, filling their cart from a single list, stopping occasionally to embrace and kiss one another – the picture of happiness and harmony. If you were to assume that these two are newly-weds enjoying a blissful morning of shopping together, I have bad news: you are a social dinosaur.

The reality is, it's long past the time when we could presume that people who appear to be married are actually so. Indeed, I do not think it would be overstating the matter to say that in the 21st century, couples who live together conjugally without actually being married are the rule rather than the exception.

Why is this so? Many answers might be offered, but I would suggest that the predominance of social utilitarianism has much to do with it. Utilitarianism, a philosophy that drives much of modern life, basically teaches that the purpose of society is to achieve the greatest good for the greatest number of people.

Applied to marriage, utilitarianism says that the purpose of the relationship is to give the couple the most possible mutual happiness. Marriage is seen as an investment whose ultimate purpose is to be profitable for both partners.

In this light, it is hardly surprising that people choose to "test drive" their conjugal relationships. After all, no wise investor would put down a cent without first determining what dividends he or she is likely to reap. Living with someone before deciding on a lifelong commitment is just good business sense…

Of course, there is a problem. A human relationship is not a business venture. People are not collections of assets to be accessed by others. When I relate to my wife, I am not merely offering one kind of happiness (financial security, for instance) in exchange for another (for instance, her maintenance of the home and care of the children).

If I relate to my wife in this way, as if she is a means to an end, then she ceases to be a person and become an object, to be used for my self-centred purposes. The utilitarian, "investment" approach to marriage, as reasonable as it first appears, is ultimately an exercise in depersonalization and dehumanization.

But if marriage is not an investment, how should we view it? In ancient societies, the answer was clear: marriage was a covenant between two people. Having agreed on the "goods" of marriage (companionship, children, stability and security), a man and a woman made a public declaration of a lifelong commitment to one another. According to the Roman definition of marriage, marriage is "the sharing of the whole of life."

The covenant view of marriage does not ask, "Why should I commit to this person? What's in it for me?" Rather, it assumes a shared set of values and publicly declares a commitment to uphold those values. When David made a covenant of friendship with Jonathan, he swore to uphold the love they already had for one another. When God made covenants with Israel, He swore to abide by His faithfulness to previous generations.

And when I make a covenant of marriage with my wife, I am swearing to uphold the values we share around our faith, childrearing beliefs, and so on. I do not ask myself how much happiness I can gain from our life together. Rather, I commit to her personally because it is good to do so, regardless of my personal happiness.

But is marriage nothing more than a covenant bond, a couple's public commitment to sharing the whole of life together?

Speaking as an Orthodox Christian, I would say that marriage must both involve and transcend such a bond. While a couple needs to be committed to values greater than their own happiness if they want to make a lasting and harmonious marriage, their ultimate goal is to make the relationship itself into an encounter with the very wellspring of their conjugal life. In short, they are called to make their marriage a *sacrament*.

According to the Orthodox Christian understanding, a sacrament is the point of intersection between God and creation. By this definition, the original Sacrament is the Person of Jesus Christ — God fully revealed in a human being. And since Jesus' humanity was the central point of God's self-revelation, all of human life (and by extension, all of the cosmos) becomes a point of encounter with God — a Sacrament.

The so-called "sacraments" of the Church are formal ways in which we proclaim and uphold the sacramental power of all life. In Baptism we claim the foundational element (water) as a meeting-place with God. In the Eucharist we claim the most basic of human activities (eating) as a way to enter God's presence.

By extension, Orthodox Christianity understands marriage in sacramental terms. Men and women are called to show forth Christ and His Church through their conjugal union and daily family life. As the couple love and serve each other, they reveal the Incarnate love of God in their domestic corner of the cosmos.

Like the rites of Baptism and the Eucharist, the rite of matrimony is a formal way in which the Church proclaims the sacramental nature of a marriage. And just as being baptised or receiving the Eucharist does not prevent a person from abandoning their faith or committing sins, the rite of matrimony itself does not achieve any transformation in a marriage; it is not magic, but rather a challenge for Christians to incarnate the presence of Jesus Christ in their marriage. How they answer that call is entirely up to them.

In other words, the sacramental view of marriage begins where the covenantal view leaves off. This is clear in the Eastern Orthodox rite of matrimony, which is conspicuously lacking a set of vows for the bride and the groom. Why? Because it is assumed and understood that the couple already know and embrace the goods of marriage and have made a covenant with one another to share the whole of life. The focus of the service lies elsewhere, on calling the couple to make their relationship a revelation of Christ.

This vocation is a profoundly personal endeavour. I am

lovingly faithful to my wife not because of the happiness I hope to gain from our relationship (as an investment), nor even because I am trying to uphold our shared values (as a covenant), but because of *who she is*, in all her uniqueness and beauty. But "who she is" is not the ultimate point either; after all, she is not an object of worship. The intimacy of our marriage leads us to encounter the One in whose image and likeness each of us was made.

The personal encounter of a sacramental marriage ultimately leads to a personal encounter with God, without losing what is unique in the bond between husband and wife. In wedding and loving each other face to face, we come face to face with the divine Bridegroom, the Lover of our souls. In being joined to one another, we experience the joining of God to humanity, of heaven to earth, in a union that will have no end.

May, 2010

The Ministry of Suffering

I was speaking recently to a colleague of mine who for the past several months has been suffering from a series of unexplained migraine headaches. At some point in the course of our conversation, he exclaimed, "How can people live this way?" It's a good question. How do we deal with the phenomenon of chronic suffering, both as sufferers and healthy loved ones who care for the afflicted?

Chronic illness and disability are a common reality. Millions of people continue to endure diabetes, MS, cancer, arthritis, Alzheimer's, depression, back pain—to mention just a few. Pain, debilitating weakness, the inability to think or speak clearly are a daily, continuing fact of life that many must negotiate.

And with no end in sight. When I get the flu, I can expect to recover. I have been forced to take a detour from the highway, but I fully anticipate rejoining the main flow in the foreseeable future. I can hardly imagine having the flu and knowing with all certainty that I will never recover from it. I won't die, but I won't get better either.

The temptation in this line of thinking, of course, is to conceive of chronic suffering as a permanent detour from normalcy. "Real life" is somewhere else, and other people are living it. The experience of the chronic sufferer, because it is not "normal," is somehow inadequate when compared to the experience of others.

According to the Gospel, however, this is just not so. Through the Incarnation, God entered the world to do away will all illness and ultimately, end all suffering: "He will wipe away every tear from their eyes, and death shall be no more, neither shall there be mourning nor crying nor pain any more, for the former things have passed away." (Rev. 21:4)

God's ultimate purpose, then, is the end of chronic suffering, including death itself. But how does He achieve that goal? He enters into suffering, fills it with Himself. He makes suffering itself the medium in which freedom is to be found.

In other words, according to the Gospel, chronic pain and illness and weakness are not a detour from real life; they are the very path leading to Real Life, which is nothing less than an encounter with the living God whose very purpose is to dwell with His people: "Behold, the dwelling of God is with men. He will dwell with them, and they shall be his people, and God himself will be with them." (Rev. 21:3)

For those of us who are generally physically healthy, it is easy to assume that the real spiritual life consists of such activities as prayer, preaching, reading the Bible, going to Church. Real ministry is overtly spiritual or religious.

If we consider the deeper implications of the Christian Gospel, however, we must realize that while some are called to obvious expressions of faith — preaching and teaching, missionary work, faithful attendance and support of their communities — many others are called simply to suffer with chronic illness and disability. In short, chronic suffering itself is a ministry, and no less so than anything else in the spiritual life.

Indeed, I would be so bold as to say that chronic suffering is the most important of all ministries. Someone who endures daily pain and weakness while trusting in the love of God, speaks far more eloquently of His power than a healthy person who, say, writes a regular article for the local newspaper...

It's one thing for a person to talk about the death and resurrection of Christ; it's another thing for him or her to live the Cross in the form of MS or cancer, while demonstrating Jesus' resurrection in his or her ongoing love for neighbour.

I would therefore urge those of us who are "healthy" to be patient with those who suffer chronically. Don't expect them to participate in obvious expressions of faith, because the fact is, they don't really need to. They are living the spiritual life more fully and really than we are, and if they even learn to endure their condition without bitterness, they will have achieved a far higher goal than we ever could.

For those who endure chronic suffering, I would say: this is your ministry. Your victory in the smallest of things — getting out of bed, being gentle with a loved one in the midst of the pain — can and will change the lives of those around you more powerfully than the most talented of writers or preachers or missionaries. It was for you above all that God entered His creation. He came to suffer not just for you, but with you and beside you. He came to go through what you are going through, so that He might see you all the way through, into a place where all sickness, sorrow and sighing will finally flee away.

July, 2010

Parenting for Faith

Seeing Us Follow

As a priest and father, it is one of my greatest hopes that my three children — Lily, Gabriel and John — would grow up to be faithful Christians. Indeed, for me, this hope exceeds all others. At this moment, I don't care what kind of work they will choose, whether they will marry or stay single, what their socioeconomic status will be — as long as they are faithful to Christ and His Church, I will be happy.

I am sure that many of you share, or have shared my aspirations in regards to your own children. And I am certain also that you have asked the question that I ask myself almost daily: how is this to be accomplished? How do I, as a parent, live and interact to ensure that my kids mature into adults of real and lasting faith?

I would be misleading you if I said that there was any sure-fire answer to that question. The very nature of Christian faith presupposes a fundamental freedom in the human person, freedom to choose or reject a relationship with Christ. Without this freedom, both God's love for us and our love for Him are meaningless.

This means simply that after we have made our best efforts to direct our children along the Way we have chosen, they must make a choice of their own, and they must continue to make that choice daily for the rest of their lives. Faith, in the Orthodox view at least, is a dynamic and continuous reality. Faith is bound up with daily faithfulness. Faith is clinging to Christ, moment by moment, and our children, once they have matured, must cling to Him by themselves, without our help or intervention.

That being said, what is our "due diligence"? How can we "speak the truth in love" (see Ephesians 4:15) to our children in the hope that they will accept our proclamation? In future articles, I will offer some guidelines to formal catechesis. Today, however, I would suggest above and beyond all educational strategies or resources, the most important factor in bringing up children as

Christians is your personal example.

In a former parish where I served, there is a man named Peter who has three teen children. Peter is an intelligent man with a straightforward, blunt, friendly personality. During my time in the parish, he assisted in the altar without fail whenever he was scheduled to do so. In addition, every Friday night, Peter prepared a large pot of chilli and every Saturday morning, he served the food to the homeless, again regularly and without fail.

Peter's children were a different story. When I arrived, they were the very embodiment of the bored teen in Church. They sat in the entryway, talking and laughing, texting on their cell phones and looking as if they would rather be anywhere but here. Sometimes the boys served, but they did so without any real enthusiasm, and I got the distinct sensation that once they were old enough to choose, they would vanish permanently.

Recently, I had the opportunity to return to my old parish for a visit. It happened that the community was holding a barbecue for the homeless at Peter's regular downtown location. When I arrived, the first person I noticed was Peter's daughter — the same one who had been sitting in a mini-skirt in the entryway, doing her nails and playing on her cell phone, bored beyond words — now enthusiastically flipping burgers and chatting with the indigent folks who lined up with their plates outstretched. I later discovered that she was also a member of the Church school staff, one of their most reliable teachers.

Now I am certain that the success I saw in Peter's daughter (I don't know about his sons) had nothing to do with how well he formally catechized his children. He is just not that kind of guy. He likes his faith simple and doesn't talk much about it. I really doubt that he spends much time speaking to his children about the tenets of their faith, telling Bible stories, or otherwise engaged in some program of education with them.

What Peter *did* do and continues to do is what I have regularly witnessed: he lives his faith in the presence of his children. And *that*, in my opinion, was the crucial element in at least one of them appropriating her faith as her own.

One of the biggest mistakes that Christian parents often make is to confuse catechism for education. We begin with the externals. Isn't there a book I can read and teach to my kids? Isn't there a curriculum I can implement? Isn't there a moral system that I can somehow drill into their little minds? We want solutions in a box, simple equations into which we can feed our kids, from which they can emerge as believers.

Now, I have nothing against formal education, curricula, moral systems, rules and so on. They have their place and I hope to discuss them in future articles. My point is, we need to get our priorities straight. Educating our children in their faith doesn't go from the outside in, but from the inside out. The words of our catechism can only be meaningful to our kids if we first *demonstrate* their meaning in our own lives.

Any commitment to becoming parents of faithful children must begin with our commitment to live as parents of faith. In reality, whether we catechize our children or not is less important than whether or not our children witness us living as obedient disciples of Jesus Christ daily. This does *not* necessarily mean that we have to be paragons of moral perfection. What we *do* need is an attitude described best in the "Big Book" of Alcoholics Anonymous: "We are willing to grow along spiritual lines... We claim spiritual progress rather than spiritual perfection." This fundamental mind-set will be crucial in determining whether or not our children will uphold us as spiritual role models and follow our path of faith.

Seeing Us Pray

Having resolved on a path of spiritual progress rather than perfection, our children should witness two basic activities in our lives. First and foremost, *they should see us praying*. This doesn't mean we need to be overtly pious. Even someone who is fumbling towards the very existence of God can be a model of prayer as they cry from the depths of their soul, "If you are out there, reveal Yourself to me!"

As long as our kids see us involved in this kind of real, consistent and honest conversation with God, we will succeed in offering them a strong witness of faith. They will come to the accurate conclusion that Dad and/or Mum are sacrificing time and effort to reach out for God, which must mean that He is somehow important...

Of course, none of this will be effective unless the optics are correct. By this I mean that we should not only be involved in the effort of regular prayer, but that our children must also *see* us in the effort of regular prayer. It won't hurt for them to "discover" you praying on one or two occasions. And if you set aside times for regular prayer, it is worth saying that you are "going to pray" within the reach of their little ears.

You may feel a bit self-conscious about exposing your prayer life like this, but remember that being a parent is a public role that involves a certain amount of staging for the good of our children. Think of all the conversations you *avoid* having in front of them and ask yourself why it is should be so strange to make personal prayer a matter of family discussion. Then consider the goal: to inculcate in your children the awareness that you are engaged in a living relationship with God. In the end, isn't it worth a little discomfort?

Seeing Us Repent

Along with seeing you pray, your children should *see you repenting daily*. As I said earlier, they will not ultimately care about your imperfections, as long as you took an attitude of willingness to grow and progress along spiritual lines. Inwardly, such growth and progress involves the effort to pray; outwardly, it involves the effort to say sorry and make amends.

A story from early Christian literature tells of a traveler in the desert who came upon a monastery. Observing the monks, who were hermits, he finally asked one of the brothers, "What is it that you do every day in your cell?" The monk replied, "We fall down, we get up. We fall down, we get up. We fall down..."

Such is the spiritual life. What counts in the end is not whether we have fallen, but whether we are struggling to rise again. As parents, this means that the most powerful witness of our faith will depend on whether or not we have the humility and the courage to "get up" by repenting of our mistakes *in the presence of our children.*

This is perhaps the most difficult parenting challenge that we will face. It means apologizing to our spouses, our colleagues, friends, acquaintances and even strangers—in plain sight of our kids. Most importantly, it means making amends to the children themselves—a humbling and even terrifying prospect.

Difficult as it may be, however, we must answer the call to be witnesses of repentance to our children. If they do not see this key piece of our spiritual life, all our prayer, all our Church attendance and external piety will count for nothing with them. They will simply dismiss us as prideful hypocrites, and rightfully so.

Seeing Us Teach

What I have said so far speaks to a foundational lesson in parenting: be a good example. There is, however, one more element involved in parenting for faith, namely, the responsibility to speak to our children about what we believe and why we believe it. In short, we must make a conscious effort to catechize our children.

Without belittling the dedicated and hardworking folks who weekly devote themselves to Christian education in their churches, I would suggest that effective catechism must primarily be rooted in a living relationship between parents and their children *in the home.* After all, if the primary witness to a child is his or her parents' own lived example, shouldn't the "talking" come from the same person who does the "walking"?

"Yes," you might say, "but I am no expert the tenets of in my faith. I am not equipped to teach my kids doctrine!"

Let me share some of my experience as a professional teacher in this regard: kids can smell B.S. long before you hand it to them. What they really want to see is someone who is honest about what they know or don't know. It's quite okay for your kids to see that you too are a student. All that they really need to know is that finding the answers is important to you, and you are confiding on leading the journey of discovery.

Whatever you do, therefore, don't pretend you are more well-informed than you really are. I guarantee they will discover your lie and your claim to be representative of the truth will be seriously undermined.

So don't worry about how expert you are. Simply embark on your own journey of learning, and having learned its lessons as thoroughly you can, pass them on as directly, honestly and as completely as possible to your children.

But what material do you choose and how do you actually teach it? With a bewildering variety of denominations, congregations and churches, not to mention claims to absolute truth throughout the Christian world, the task of finding a catechesis is overwhelming. However, it need not be so. Assuming a generally Christian context (the only one I am familiar with), I would suggest that the foundation for sound doctrine of any sort is a complete and deeply-rooted knowledge of the Old and New Testaments.

Don't get me wrong here: I am not saying that Scripture should be sole source of a child's doctrinal knowledge. As I have said before, Scripture is not self-interpreting and must be read and understood within a living framework of worship and spiritual practice — what Eastern Orthodox Christianity would call *tradition*.

Before a child can appropriate the proper interpretation of Scripture in tradition, however, he or she must first grasp *what* is being interpreted — the scriptural material from which tradition is wrought. To put it briefly, we can't understand who Christ is "according to the Scriptures" unless we first know the Scriptures that ultimately point to Him!

In this view, I am not alone. The great 4th century preacher and teacher, John Chrysostom, offers similar advice in his homily, *Address on Vainglory and the Right Way for Parents to Bring Up Their Children*. Comparing the soul of a child to city and parents to lawmakers and rulers, Chrysostom emphasizes the importance of one of the city's "gates"—the ears—by which "thoughts are corrupted or rightly guided."

How to protect this particular gate in the soul of a child? Chrysostom's prescription is twofold. Firstly, protect your child from stories that teach vices. He offers one example: "Such and such a girl kissed such and such a man, and had no luck and hanged herself." In other words, Chrysostom urges us to prevent our children from hearing stories in which people are involved in the destruction of their souls.

For us, this means setting clear and firm boundaries about what books our children will read, what movies or TV shows they will see, what web sites they will visit, or what music they will listen to—itself a daunting challenge.

Secondly, Chrysostom urges that we offer our children stories from the Scripture. He tells us specifically how this should be done:

1. Establish a context in which to establish a family storytelling tradition. Chrysostom advocates for an evening meal at which the whole family is gathered.
2. Choose a story, such as that of Cain and Abel and having learned it thoroughly yourself, begin in the classic way: "Once upon a time." At this stage, you need not insist on chapter and verse. The point is to teach the stories first, and only later to teach how they relate to one another in the wider scope of the Scriptures.

3. Elaborate the story with relevant and appropriate details to engage the child's mind. Include probable character motivations, as well as interpretations true to basic doctrinal teaching, e.g. Abel was received into heaven.
4. Draw out simple, clear lessons from the story, e..g. the futility of Cain's attempts to conceal his sins from God.
5. Repeat the story for several nights and then ask the child to tell *you* the story in his or her own way.
6. Provide the child with an opportunity to hear the story read and preached on in Church. In the Orthodox tradition, this would also involve them hearing hymnography that would interpret the story in the light of doctrine.

Whether we are able to follow Chrysostom's prescriptions exactly is not of vital importance. The larger point is clear. If we make a start at living lives of faith for our own salvation and as an example to our children, if we establish with them a foundation by which they can understand that life of faith through the regular telling of stories from Scripture, then we will have already gone a long way to parenting children who will hold fast to Christ, not just until their dying breath, but beyond, into the age to come.

January-February, 2010

The Principle of Dispassion

As a priest and a pastor, I am particularly susceptible to a temptation known as "the Saviour complex." This is the belief that I possess god-given abilities, powers and charismas to manage and fix other people's lives.

My "stinking thinking" goes like this: if I can be compassionate and kind enough to others, if I can devote enough time and energy to them, if I can preach or teach well enough, then I can lift those in my care above the chaos and destruction of their lives. Like some kind of spiritual Superman I can fly in and save the day!

It's pretty obvious that such an attitude is personally destructive. When an ordinary human being is deluded into thinking he possesses the personal power to singlehandedly redeem another, something has gone terribly wrong. He has succumbed to a blasphemy of the worst sort—the belief that he is a god, able to direct the destinies of lesser mortals. You can imagine what happens to this poor creature when he is unable to meet his own exalted expectations and comes crashing down to earth again...

Yes, the problems with the Saviour complex are pretty clear. To quote a character from *Corner Gas*, "It's not rocket surgery." And yet I am not the only one who falls prey to these kinds of temptations. *All of us* who would actively practice our faith by regularly serving others can fall prey to the delusion that the salvation of those whom we serve rests on the extent and extra-ordinariness of our personal resources.

Does the transformation of human lives involve our gifts and efforts? Absolutely. The Apostle Paul says simply, "Bear one another's burdens and so fulfil the law of Christ." (Gal. 6:2) In addition, the Gospel offers almost countless injunctions and examples that predicate our salvation on mutual love and service.

But where does healthy involvement in the acts of charity

towards our neighbours degenerate into the conviction that their eternal destinies depend on us and our efforts? How do we draw the line between simply obeying Jesus' commands, and using those commands as an opportunity to stroke our own egos?

In response, I would like to share a story from the Eastern Orthodox tradition.

Mother Gavrila was well-known for her personal holiness and her care for all those who visited her. Day in and day out, visitors would come to her, so that there were often line ups for hours outside her monastic cell. The other nuns who observed these visits noted that while the visitor was present, Mother Gavrila would be so focused upon them, that the rest of the world would disappear. She would ignore both her own needs and the needs of the bystanders, making the concerns and sufferings of her visitor the centre of everything—laughing with them, weeping with them, suffering just as they did.

When the visitor departed, however, Mother Gavrila would go to the corner where she prayed and offer a few words of intercession for that person. Then she would forget about them. The burdens she had carried during the visit were lifted from her. She was light-hearted again, ready to make the next visitor the centre of her attention.

Mother Gavrila's behaviour could, on first inspection, seem rather callous. In reality, though, she demonstrates the principle of dispassion, which is crucial to anyone who serves God by serving other human beings.

Ultimately, we are stewards of the things God has given us. Our gifts, abilities, ministries, belong to Him, and we are only entrusted with them for a time, charged to use them for His glory until He returns and calls us to account.

When we are called to perform a task or serve a person, that task or person must be central. We must prepare for the encounter with as much care as we can muster. When we get on with the task, all of our enthusiasm, effort, and emotion must be devoted to its completion—just as Mother Gavrila did.

Once the task is complete or the person leaves our presence, however, Mother Gavrila's story reminds that it is time to commend them to God and disconnect from the effort. Whatever happened was ordered by God and accomplished according to His will. What He chooses to do with that event is in His hands, not ours.

Our challenge, then, is to simply offer what is past to Him and be done with it. If we made a mistake, we can amend it if or when the opportunity presents itself again, with as much consideration as *anything* set before us in the present moment.

Mother Gavrila's dispassion is not by any means callousness or indifference. Agonizing over the destinies of others, however good-intentioned, is nothing more than pride, pure and simple. When people come before us, we serve and love them to the extent we are able in that moment. When they leave our sphere of activity, we relinquish them to the only One who controls their destinies— the real God and Saviour.

I was once told, "The ultimate significance of your life is none of your business." Remembering that piece of advice— remembering to live simply as a creature, a servant, a steward—is difficult and challenging enough. We hardly need to take on the burden of controlling our own fate, let alone that of the rest of humanity.

February, 2010

More on Dispassion

On first appearance, Dispassion seems to be a negative quality; we tend to associate it with coldness, lack of emotion or concern, and even inhumanity. A closer look at this word, however, reveals something deeper in its meaning. "Dispassion" is a Latin rendition of the Greek word "apatheia," which is the negative form of the word for "suffering." To be dispassionate, then, means literally "not to suffer."

But let's take this a little further. Originally, "suffering" referred to the condition of being subject to something beyond our control. We still hear vestiges of this meaning in phrases like "Bob suffered a heart attack." It's not just that Bob's heart attack was painful; more accurately, the heart attack came upon him and *there was nothing he could do about it.*

When I drop a pencil on the floor, it "suffers," not because it "hurt itself" on impact, but because it could not resist the force of gravity that pulled it inevitably downward. Suffering is slavery to something outside ourselves, whether it is a force like gravity, a dimension like time, or a condition like a heart attack.

Holding this definition in mind, then, we can say that dispassion — lack of suffering — is the quality of not being enslaved to external impulses. When acted on by an outside agent, we do not simply *react*, like a pencil drawn downward by gravity, but remain fundamentally in control of our response to the situation.

Here's another story from the Eastern Orthodox tradition to illustrate.

Pachomius was an elder living in the desert. One day, a young man came to visit him and asked, "Abba, what can I do to be saved?"

The old man thought for a moment, then said, "Go to the cemetery and curse the gravestones."

The young man was puzzled, but he obeyed. He went to the cemetery and shouted the worst curses he could imagine at the gravestones. When he returned, Pachomius said, "Now go back and praise the tombs to the sky."

The young man again obeyed, feeling rather foolish. When he returned the second time, the Elder asked, "Now tell me: when you yelled curses at the graves, what did they say?"

"Nothing," the young man replied, still not knowing where this was going.

"And when you praised them, what was their response?"

"Nothing, Abba. They were silent."

"If you would be saved," Pachomius said, "you must become like the gravestones, being moved neither by men's curses nor their praise."

In this story, Pachomius was not suggesting that the young man become void of feeling, his heart as hard as a gravestone. He would certainly say that emotions are an integral part of who we are, and that to deny them is to deny our very humanity.

Rather, the Elder was exhorting his protégé to become free from enslavement to external forces. However good or bad something may feel, he is suggesting, you cannot allow that feeling to control how you respond. Having a feeling is perfectly natural and good; being controlled by that feeling is something else entirely.

It comes down to this: if someone behaves like a jerk and I feel like punching his lights out, do I act on it? Or do I heed the Psalmist's advice: "Be angry, but sin not; commune with your own hearts on your beds, and be silent" (Ps. 4:4)? When someone hurts me unjustly, do I react as my feelings would dictate, or do I follow Jesus and say, "Father, forgive them; for they know not what they do" (Luke 23:24)?

The right choice seems clear. And yet our society would have us follow our feelings blindly, making choices according to our least whim and impulse. Advertisers count on precisely this kind of reaction when they bombard our senses with their sounds and images. Faced with such an onslaught, dispassion is the answer.

Indeed, I would go even further and say that acquiring dispassion is the most important and urgent challenge of the spiritual life. If we want to mediate true spiritual healing in this world of ours, each of us needs to seek freedom from those forces — biological, psychological, emotional, social, national, ideological and even religious — that would subject us to their wills and ultimately, pit us against one another.

When something comes into our orbit and threatens to throw off our equilibrium — whether towards the negative or the positive — we cannot allow it dictate our actions or reactions. Instead, we must offer everything — however bad or good it feels — to God, allowing *Him* and Him alone to measure our best response.

In the remaining days of Lent, therefore, I pray you would strive towards acquiring a greater measure of dispassion, for in this attitude you are guaranteed to find the key to inner peace, freedom, and a truly happy existence.

March, 2010

The Sanctity of Human Life

This week, many Christian churches throughout North America will celebrate the Sanctity of Human Life in protest of the ongoing prevalence of legalized abortion in our society. My goal in this article is not to enter into this controversial debate, but simply to present the Orthodox position on the moral and legal issues around abortion.

The Orthodox Christian Church has always asserted that life begins at conception. Numerous written proofs aside, the Church calendar celebrates both birthdays and conception days. Most well-known is March 25th, when Christ was conceived by the Holy Spirit of the Virgin Mary at the Annunciation. Significantly, this celebration takes place nine months before Christ's birth on December 25th... In addition, we also celebrate the conceptions of Saint John the Baptist (September 23rd) and Mary the Mother of God (December 9th).

The sanctity of conception flows from the Orthodox teaching that God creates all of us in His image and likeness from the beginning: "For You formed my inward parts, You knitted me together in my mother's womb." (Ps. 139:13) Our dignity as human beings does not primarily derive from national citizenship upon birth. Rather, we possess inherent value and worth because God loved us and cared for us and called us His children from the very instant He granted us the spark of life at conception.

Following on this logic, the Church has always condemned the conscious and wilful act of destroying the foetus as the taking of a human life. Basil the Great, a Church father writing in the 4th century, puts it very bluntly: "A woman who deliberately destroys a foetus is answerable for murder. And any fine distinction between its being completely formed or unformed is not admissible among us."

No doubt many of you have by now labelled me a hard-line conservative, placing me on one side of a battle in which clear lines have been drawn. On one side are those who argue for the legal precedence of a woman's rights over that of the foetus she carries in her womb. They assert that the state is not subject to the morality of the Church, but must represent the interests of all its citizens, religious and non-religious alike.

On the other side are those who affirm basically what I have said, but go on to argue that the laws legalizing abortion should be repealed on the basis that they condone murder. They argue that both the United States and Canada were founded on Christian principles, the laws must reflect those principles if they are to be true to their identity.

As morally conservative as I am, I would like to take a "third way" on the issue of legislation. The Orthodox Church has always held that, in the words of one prayer, the state exists to "provide peace that Your holy Church and all Your people may calm and ordered in all godliness and sanctity." As long as the Church and its members are able to continue "working out their salvation" (see Phi. 2:12) in peace, the state can use whatever political system is expedient to meet the needs of its citizenry.

It is for this reason that the Orthodox Church has been willing (if not always able) to exist under the Roman and Ottoman Empires, in Tsarist Russia, under Communism, not to mention socialism and democracy in their various forms. Although the Church has always welcomed Christian impulses in its civil authorities, it has never demanded that they institute a theocracy of any kind. It has simply asked them to provide a space of peace in which it can conduct its life of faith and worship.

The Orthodox Church in North America now lives in a democracy, which has as its basic mandate equal representation for all citizens, believers and non-believers alike. If our civil leaders wish to be elected to office, they must guarantee such representation, regardless of their personal creed. This is the dilemma of the Christian politician. He or she must champion the will of their constituency, even if that will contradicts his or her own fundamental principles. Otherwise, they must forfeit their office.

The simple reality of democracy is "majority rules." And the majority of Canadian citizens are not opposed to legal abortion. As a Christian, I may vehemently disagree with them, but I accept the democratic process as the least imperfect system for the attaining peace and harmony in 21st century. So as long as democracy allows the Church to continue to live in faith, I will continue to live with democracy, if uncomfortably and with a sense of outrage at its many moral failings, including its failure to protect its unborn citizens.

Am I failing my duty as a Christian? Should I not be fighting every day to build a Christian nation? As an Orthodox Christian, I feel no imperative to re-establish a theocracy and legislate my beliefs, because I do not believe that the Church depends on legislation to build the Kingdom of God. Mere legislation at best cuts off the poisonous flower of evil; it cannot reach its dark roots, which feed off the basic spiritual ailment of our society: the devaluation of the human person created in the image and likeness of God.

And so this Christian will continue to fight the war against evil and build the Kingdom of God, not on Parliament hill, but on another battleground: the individual hearts and minds of men and women, who by God's grace repent and commit their lives to Christ one a time, and strive to make different choices for true life in Him, one day at a time.

January, 2009

The Faithful Ones

Recently, it was my great joy to attend a kind of celebration so rare in our time that it deserves an entire article devoted to it: the 50th anniversary of the loving marriage between two faithful Christians.

Paul and Jeannette Mentenko have a special place in my heart. I regard them as elders on my own spiritual journey. My wife and I look up to them as examples of a loving Christian marriage that has endured and continues to thrive. As a priest, I see them as paradigms of true lay service in a Christian community.

Noteworthy as this couple is, though, their golden anniversary celebration was characteristically understated. A few of the Church ladies cooked the supper, which consisted of ham, turkey, mashed potatoes and veggies. Dessert was a wedding cake baked by a friend. The drinks came in plastic cups, the food on paper plates.

The entertainment was equally unpretentious. Paul and a friend did a duet on fiddle and guitar. My wife and daughter sang "Bound for the Promised Land." Another old friend of the couple (who herself had just celebrated her 51st wedding anniversary) told some jokes. It felt like an open mike at a family reunion.

One of the highlights of the evening came when Paul got up and spoke to his wife in terms of tenderness and endearment that brought tears to our eyes. Following this, our own Archbishop Seraphim, who was seated at the centre of the head table, awarded Paul and Jeannette a *grammata*, a traditional certificate recognizing their past and continuing years of faithful lay service to the Church.

Leaving this simple and down-to-earth event, I was struck with a sense of having witnessed something both beautiful and dignified: two lives of steadfast faith lived in complete and loving union for over five decades.

You might ask, as I did, how they managed it? If you think that Paul and Jeannette had it easy in some way, you would be wrong. Financial struggles and hardships dogged them for years, and now they live without savings on their Canada pensions alone. They suffered too in the raising of their children, with every kind of sorrow about which they were often helpless to do anything, except pray. And no doubt, they worked through the familiar daily difficulties involved in a working marriage.

18 years ago, Jeannette had a kidney transplant. Ever since, she has struggled with the anti-rejection medications, often being so debilitated that she is confined to her bed. Heart attacks, bouts of pneumonia, countless operations — these are some of the sufferings Jeannette has endured, with Paul steadfast by her side.

In other words, their life together has been no easier or more ideal than anyone else's; and more often than not, it has been more difficult. Yet Paul and Jeannette have maintained their marriage in love and faithfulness to each other, while preserving their belief that God holds their relationship in His providential hands.

Are these people somehow "super" Christians, possessing extraordinary inner resources that allowed them to weather the storm? Perhaps, but it's unlikely. From what I know of their personal spiritual lives, I am aware that they have cultivated the habit of praying daily for everyone they know. I recall, for instance, visiting them and seeing a photograph of myself and my family hanging with several others in the corner where they go to pray — reminders of those whom they commit to God's care every day.

And what of the *grammatta*, the certificate that the Archbishop presented in honour of Paul and Jeannette's exemplary service to the Church? For Paul, exemplary service means the temple regularly, and restocking candles and supplies. For Jeannette, it is even more fundamental: she attends and contributes to every Church event that her weakened body will permit. They are just faithful people, who over the years have continually supported and encouraged their leaders and their community as best they could. Their choice to seat the Archbishop at the centre of their head table was more than merely accidental. For Paul and Jeannette, Christ and His Church are always the centre of everything.

I have told this dear couple's story, because in my limited experience, there is no shortage of those who long for power and glory in Church, who are zealous to improve and fix and reshape communities according to their personal vision. There is no end to the line of people who enjoy titles and honours, who would like their names on plaques, who dream of being toasted at banquets and applauded by congregations.

But extraordinary indeed arc people like Paul and Jeannette, people who do not obtrude, who struggle quietly and are victorious without fanfare; who serve in whatever capacity they are needed—no matter how simple and lowly the task—cheerfully and steadfastly and without complaint. Rare indeed are the people who accept whatever life God gives them, offering up everything and everyone they encounter to Him.

Don't get me wrong; we need leaders, visionaries, movers and shakers. But as we seek to raise up those folks to stand in the limelight, let's not forget to honour and treasure those in the wings, who come early and stay late without being asked; who encourage without fail; who can always be called upon on in a pinch; who are cheerful, prayerful, and humble. Let's not forget the faithful ones; they are truly worthy of our praise.

July, 2009

Three Lessons from the Salvation Army

For two and a half years until this past December, it was my honour and joy to work part-time at the Salvation Army in Cranbrook.

Originally, I sought and found the job out of necessity; I needed some "secular" employment to supplement my salary as the priest of St. Aidan's. As the months and now years have passed, however, I have seen in retrospect the hand of God tracing His usual glorious design in my life. What was a desperate bid to make ends meet I now see as an opportunity to rediscover the essentials of following Christ through my love for my neighbour.

My Salvation Army job is relatively easy to describe. My official title was "Community Ministry worker," and I solved problems. If you were fleeing an abusive relationship and had left all your belongings behind, I provided you with clothes, furniture, and household items. If you were homeless and the shelters were closed, I provided tents and sleeping bags. If you were on a limited food budget and your Food Bank allocation had run out, I provided emergency hampers. If you were having legal troubles and needed a consultation, I referred you to a pro bono lawyer. And so on.

If at this point you are tempted to conjure softly-lit scenes involving sentimental music and possibly a halo, let me enlightenment you right now. I worked 14 hours a week at a reasonable hourly rate, and during that time, I did what is required of me, no less and not much more. Now I am no longer in that office, someone else is, doing the same job as well (or better) than I did it.

That being said, this job was a real education for me, by which I mean it has taught me some painful and difficult but ultimately valuable spiritual lessons. I will share the three that stand out for me.

Lesson #1: Serve without expectations. If you work long enough in a place like the Salvation Army, whether as a volunteer or as an employee, you soon discover that people often go through cycles, especially if addiction is involved. Recovery and relapse follow each other in a seemingly endless procession, and only after long periods of time do some begin to demonstrate anything like progress.

Why people change for the better is a mystery—God working in ways we cannot perceive. One thing is certain: people like me who doled out clothing vouchers and food hampers are not primarily responsible.

If you serve the poor in some capacity once a year around Christmas by say, helping with the Christmas Kettles (and yes, that is a hint to sign up as a volunteer this year), it's easy to miss this important truth. And if you choose to serve regularly, the frustration of our human tendency to repeat the same mistakes again and again can lead you to disillusion, despair, or worse yet, indifference.

The real trick lies in ridding ourselves of expectations. Too often we serve the poor and needy with the expectation that we are actually going to help or improve them. In reality, we discover that only God can help and "improve" others, and then only in His own time and manner. Our task is simply to do what He asks us to do for those in need, *just because He asked us to do it*, and leave the changing of hearts and minds up to the only One who can accomplish such changes.

Lesson #2: Recognize Jesus in everyone. One of the Fathers of the Church, Maximos the Confessor, once said, "The poor man is God." Behind this is the Eastern Orthodox understanding that when God united human nature to Himself in the Person of Jesus Christ, He made it possible for us to meet and serve Him whenever we encounter humanity in the person of our neighbour.

Often, our neighbour has something to offer us in return for our service: friendship, money, psychological affirmation, emotional security, and so on. The 'poor man,' however, has nothing to offer. When we love and serve someone in utter need, we do so purely out of obedience to God. In that sense, Maximos is correct: the 'poor man' is God in a way the 'rich man' is not, because the needy more fully reveal God's presence to us than those who can reward our service.

As the Community Ministry worker at the Salvation Army, I received some recompense for my service. Believe me when I say, however, there were many times when the service far exceeded the rather modest compensation ... And it was during those times I learned to 'recognize Jesus in everyone,' to treat the needs of the person in front of me as if God Himself was asking for a food hamper or a clothing voucher or some advocacy with the Ministry of Social Services. In the end, there is no other (or better) reason for serving the poor.

Lesson #3: Seek times of sanctuary. The Salvation Army can be a very busy place and at times, the busyness can threaten to overflow into every spare minute of a day. As a part-time staff member, I was nowhere near as busy as those in charge, but as a priest, I am all too aware of just how all consuming this work can become.

In this regard, I have learned to be grateful for the opportunities for sanctuary afforded by the Orthodox Christian tradition: the daily Matins and Vespers services, the practice of quiet prayer known as Hesychia ('the Way of Inner Stillness'). In addition, I have come to cherish my day off every week, during which I spend time with my wife and children, resting and recharging.

I have learned that just as important as the giving of one time, energy and resources to others, is the taking of time to drink from the wellspring of life, in God and in those whom He has given us as a support and a help. Without my work at the Salvation Army, I may have learned that lesson the hard way, or not learned it at all. But I am discovering as I go along that my God has a way of acting in unexpected and surprising ways for my joy and salvation, and for that, I am grateful.

March, 2011

Worship as Sacrifice

Recently, the pastor of another community, a man for whom I have the greatest respect, invited my parishioners and I to celebrate a Sunday morning service with his congregation. Sadly, I had to decline. The reasons for this were firstly practical. Combining two very different kinds of services—one Eastern Orthodox, the other Protestant—without losing the integrity of each would prove too difficult, if not impossible.

The other issue, though, was more profound. Before he and I could even face the complications of combining style and content, we would have to face the fact that our very definitions of what constitutes worship are different. Without this common understanding, what would it even mean to 'worship' together, anyway?

Is worship praise and song, as in hymns or choruses? Is worship preaching and teaching, as in a sermon or a testimonial? Is worship prayer, as in praying collectively for others or the world? Does worship involve Eucharistic communion? If you had just a sermon, or just hymns or just communal prayer by themselves, would it still be worship, or does worship require certain elements to be deemed worship?

These are questions many Christians have grappled with for at least five hundred years. Various answers have been put forward, resulting in the current plethora of Christian practices across the denominational spectrum.

Faced with this diversity (some might call it confusion), many choose to respond in the spirit of religious pluralism. Too frequently, people visiting Saint Aidan's have said to me, "We all worship the same God, but it's so nice to see other styles of worship..." Frankly, this is a cop out. Confronted by differences in worship and not wanting to deal with the issues, we tend to become vague and fuzzy, and simply choose to believe that because a group of people gather together, sing, pray and listen to a teaching or meditation, they must be engaging in worship, whatever its flavour. If the definition is vague enough, we believe, then we will all get along and live happily ever after.

I wish that were true. The fact is, Christians and indeed all people of faith, cannot worship together meaningfully or effectively unless they have come to a consensus on what it is exactly they are doing. To simply assemble and perform a common order of service together, without really agreeing on what is happening, and to call the result 'worshiping together' is just not accurate. Diners in a Smorgasbord restaurant may be eating food in the same place, but to what extent are they sharing a communal meal?

No, the question of what exactly is worship must be faced and answered if people of faith are ever going to worship together. The solution, in my opinion, is not that complicated. We must return to our common roots. If we believe in a God who is unchanging, shouldn't the worship of that God also be essential unchanging? Indeed, for as long as our race has existed, human beings have understood worship as possessing a very specific characteristic that bears rediscovering in our own communities: sacrifice.

Worship has always been sacrificial. Put in simple terms, the reasoning behind this is as follows:

A) Something is wrong with the world as it is, and we are somehow responsible.

B) There is some Power beyond our own capable of restoring things to their proper   state.

C) We offer that Power something crucial to our own lives, to demonstrate our dependence on divine intervention.

This is sacrifice. We give up something important (usually the food and drink that keeps us alive, or else the time and the money that allows us to provide for the basic needs of ourselves and our families), so that we can demonstrate that we need divine intervention to restore, fulfil, and preserve our lives.

Sacrifice is an affirmation that God is God, and we are not.

When we sacrifice, we come to the Power greater than ourselves and give up things that are important to us in the hope that this God will respond by taking care of us. The act of sacrificing is painful and difficult, and it should be. It feels like death, because it is.

Whatever else worship is (and much more may be said), it is first and foremost <u>sacrifice</u>. Too regularly, I see churches catering to their congregations, making God attractive, palatable and easy to digest, with more comfortable or pleasant surroundings and activities, softer and less challenging messages, and greater perks for attendance (would you like a Grande Latte and pastry with that sermon?).

If we are ever to make a start on the journey back to truly worshiping the same God, we first need to agree that worship involves people coming to God on His terms, not Him coming to us on our terms. Worship should not be a comfortable experience. It should deprive us of vital resources. It should challenge and drain us, leaving us empty and ready to receive the life that God alone has to give.

The desert elders of the Eastern Orthodox tradition have a saying: "Give God your blood and He will give you His spirit." Hard as it may be to hear, the true worship of God demands a total sacrifice of ourselves, our comforts and conveniences, our assumptions and agendas. Any less an effort is simply our backhanded way of saying that God is just not worth the effort because He is not really the ultimate Giver of life. Worshiping God, or denying God—maybe it's time to take a closer look at what we're really doing.

May, 2010

A Taste of the Fullness

A Third Way of Reading the Bible

When it comes to reading the Bible, two distinct schools of thought seem to exist. On one hand, there's the 'Literal' school of biblical interpretation, which generally takes any given text from the Bible and upholds its literal historical meaning as the incontrovertible truth. If it is says so in the Bible, then that's how it happened and that's how it is.

In apparent contrast to this Literal school of biblical is the 'Liberal' school. Liberal interpreters generally assert that Scripture is really just myth and allegory. When reading the Bible, they say, we cannot take the surface meaning as the 'Gospel truth.' The Bible is, after all, a religious document, not a historical one. Its meaning is to be understood in purely symbolic terms, for its spiritual or metaphorical meaning.

It would seem that the Literals and the Liberals stand on opposite sides of biblical interpretation debate. In fact, the two approaches are really two sides of the same coin. Whether you are Literal or Liberal, you are still working with the same basic assumption that the meaning of the Scriptures centres around the question of historical veracity. For the Literals, the historical accuracy of the Scriptures makes them true. For the Liberals, the historical inaccuracy of Scriptures is the basis of their 'symbolic' truth. Either way, the historicity of the text is both the starting point and the destination of the debate.

May I suggest a third way? I like to call it the 'prophetic' method, but it's nothing new. This manner of interpreting the Bible has been practiced within the body of Eastern Orthodox theology for almost two thousand years.

The basic assumption of prophetic exegesis derives from the New Testament, in which the risen Christ appears to His disciples on the road to Emmaus. *Beginning with Moses and all the prophets, he interpreted to them in all the scriptures the things concerning himself.*

(Luke 24:27. See also John 5:46)

The entire purpose of the Scriptures, then, is to lead us to Christ. The Old Testament is ultimately a foreshadowing of the fulfillment of God's plan of salvation in the Son of God. The goal of interpreting the Scriptures is to encounter Christ Himself. The meaning of the text is not primarily historical or symbolical; it is *personal*.

The prophetic method thus begins with the guiding interpretative principle that whatever text we encounter in the Scriptures, it *must* lead us to the Person of Christ and *must* be interpreted as a prophecy of Him.

Allow me to demonstrate how this works. First, let's take one of many 'difficult' texts in Scripture: *O daughter of Babylon, you destructive one! Happy shall he be who requites you with what you have done to us! Happy shall he be who takes your little ones and dashes them against the rock!* (Psalm 137:8-9)

Asked to justify this horrific image, a Literal interpreter might shrug and say, "That's the Old Testament. We are no longer bound by the law, which says that God *will by no means clear the guilty, visiting the iniquity of fathers upon children, upon the third and upon the fourth generation.* (Numbers 14:18) *We* live under grace."

Confronting the same text, a Liberal might respond with a grimace: "That's the Old Testament. It reflects the clan mentality of primitive cultures. It's no longer relevant today. Jesus calls us to live with mercy and tolerance for our enemies."

So from both points of view, the text is effectively dead. It has no power and significance in my life as a Christian here and now.

How does the prophetic method handle these verses? It begins on the literal, historical level. The killing of infants does indeed reflect the ancient Near Eastern understanding that the crime of one generation was carried forward to future generations. So it makes sense that the Israelites would seek to utterly annihilate their Babylonian enemies.

If our interpretation stopped there, we would have little more than an archaeological curiosity, an example of an outdated and barbaric practice. But the prophetic method continues to ask, how do these verses prophecy to Christ? The response: the 'rock' refers to Christ, the Rock of our salvation. (see Psalm 18:2 and 1 Corinthians 10:4) The 'little ones' dashed against this rock refer to sinful passions, which we are called to 'dash,' which is to say, put to death *at the moment of their birth in our minds and hearts.*

So the prophetic method is neither Literal nor Liberal. It does not ignore the historical level of the Scriptures: if we did not understand the nature of clan vengeance, the meaning of the verses would be lost. But neither does it stay on the Literal level, otherwise the verses would be irrelevant for us today. Rather, the method goes on to interpret them metaphorically, as symbolizing Christ and the crucifixion of our sinful passions.

In the end, the prophetic method always makes the chosen text spiritually fresh, relevant and powerful. It leads us into the Scriptures, through the Scriptures from the literal to the spiritual, and beyond, to the fulfillment of the Scriptures in the *personal relationship* with Christ. The ultimate goal of reading the Scriptures is to meet the One of whom the Scriptures speaks, whom the disciples met on the road to Emmaus, whom they knew in the breaking of the bread, whom they proclaimed and delivered to the following generations in their writings, preaching and traditions. (see 1 Corinthians 11:2 and 2 Thessalonians 2:15)

In contrast to the well-worn and tired methods of Literalism or Liberalism, I offer the prophetic method as a third way for your consideration and the further enrichment your continuing study of the Bible. For generations since the road to Emmaus, Eastern Orthodox exegetes have used it to fruitfully interpret everything from Genesis to Revelation. May it also bear fruit in your life and become a source of joy and refreshment for your soul.

March 2009

The *One* Church

In the Creed of Nicaea-Constantinople (known as the Nicene Creed), the Christian Church is described as "one, holy, catholic, and apostolic." In the next few weeks, I would like reflect from an Eastern Orthodox angle on the meanings of these words, and what they tell us about the nature of the Church as a whole.

I will begin today with the first descriptor of the Church: that it is "one."

It is no secret that, much like Christian communities all over the world, the Christian communities in Cranbrook are a divided bunch. The proverbial Martian descending on our town for the first time would discover the Roman Catholic Church, the Orthodox Church, Baptists, Lutherans, the United Church, Anglicans, and numerous evangelical Protestant denominations: Alliance, Foursquare Gospel, Salvation Army, Pentecostal, as well as various independent groups of different stripes.

After further inquiry, our Martian visitor would discover that the churches of Cranbrook don't have much to do with one another, other than a couple of joint yearly events. Our interplanetary inquirer would learn that there is a Ministerial Association comprised of pastors, priests and ministers who have agreed to meet and pray and sometimes work together, without looking too closely at their doctrinal differences.

Then there's another group, called "the Net," a group not affiliated with the Cranbrook Ministerial Association, who also meet and pray and work together among themselves regularly. And finally, there are a handful of ministers who have nothing to do with either the Ministerial or "the Net." In short, the proverbial Martian, search as he might, would be hard put to see anything like "one" Church in the city of Cranbrook.

I will say it out loud: this situation is abhorrent, scandalous, and tragic. But what is the solution? What is the true basis of Christian unity?

The problem, I believe, is that different Christian communities use different criteria to define the meaning of unity. The Roman Catholic Church defines unity on the basis of communion with the authority of the Roman see expressed in the office of the Pope. It is an institutional unity in which doctrine and faith are defined from a central source.

Many Protestant denominations, by contrast, define unity on the basis of the Bible. For them, Christians are not "a people under the Pope," but "a people under the Book." As long as one holds to the inerrant authority of the Bible, one is united to others who believe likewise, thereby constituting the Church.

Still others take a more confession-based approach. They concede that not everyone interprets the Bible in the same way, but as long as you confess that "Jesus is Lord," you are part of a vast, universal body of believers who confess the same thing. And, to take it one step further, there are some Christians who go even farther, defining unity on the basis of belief in God generally, whether He is manifested in Jesus or not.

All of these approaches are, I believe, problematic. The jurisdictional unity under a centralized authority in Rome may be useful in regards to discipline and order, but its claim to be a unifying doctrinal force among Christians is founded on the assumption that when the papacy speaks formally, it is incapable of error in doctrine. This claim to infallibility is a position that I and others find difficult to accept.

Using the Bible as the sole basis of the one Church, however, is equally hazardous. Foundational as the Bible is to Christian faith, it has not proven itself adequate as the *sole* means to Christian unity. If this were so, why are there literally tens of thousands of competing denominations, all of whom claim to be interpreting the same text correctly? The problem with basing a faith on a scriptural text *alone* is that the text must be interpreted, but who interprets, and whose interpretation is authoritative?

Why then can't we just define the Church by the simple

confession that "Jesus is Lord"? Or why can't we go even further and talk about unity among religions in which God is made known in different ways, Jesus being one of those ways? If we define commonality of belief in general enough terms, isn't that enough?

It may be for some, but not for me. I may call Jesus "Lord," but so did Arius, a fourth century teacher who also proposed that Jesus was not really and fully God, but a quasi-divine being created at some point before the creation of the world. Another teacher, Nestorius, also called Jesus "Lord," but he also said that Mary did not give birth to God in the flesh, but that Jesus assumed his divine identity later, when He came of age. These are not differences over which I can agree to "live and let live," for they each result in completely irreconcilable conceptions of Jesus, none of whom I recognize as Saviour.

And as for defining unity in still more general terms that allow for other personal revelations of God other than Jesus, what can I say? If the Apostles and the martyrs of the early Church were content with that understanding, why would they rather be tortured and killed than confess that *anyone* else but Jesus was the full revelation God Himself? Why didn't they simply admit that God was revealed in the Emperor, just as He was in Jesus? Do we really want to follow a Christ other than the One who was confessed by the Apostles who knew Him and the martyrs who gave up their lives for His sake?

So again we must ask, what is the solution to Christian unity? And again, I must say: I do not know. But I can say that we must begin with the person of Jesus Christ. As Fr. John Behr, a contemporary Orthodox theologian, has said: "*Christ* is the subject of Christian theology," which means *He* is the only real foundation of Christian unity. By clinging to "one Lord" through our "one baptism," we also come to share "one faith" in the one Body of the Church. (see Eph. 4:4-16) Just as the spokes on a bicycle wheel converge at the hub, so too are we united in our common union with the same Jesus Christ.

It's a simple point, but one we have missed to a greater or lesser extent. If we are going to take the first baby steps towards real Christian unity, I believe that we need to find a concrete and comprehensive and unified answer to the question that He asked His own disciples: "Who do you say that I am?" (Mark 8:29)

To merely recite the phrase, "He is fully God and fully man," is not sufficient. After all, what do those words *mean*? Do they mean He is a schizophrenic Christ: two disassociated persons in one body? Or is He some kind of God-man blend — a superman ultimately alien from ordinary human experience? All of these questions are not merely abstract points of debate. They have real and serious repercussions on how God has made Himself known to us, and how we relate both to Him and to one another.

I would therefore encourage you to make a personal beginning at answering Jesus' fundamental question: "Who do you say that I am?" For at least the first thousand years of its history, Christians struggled to respond, and the fruits of their labours are well-documented and freely available online (check out www.ccel.org). A good place to start is Athanasius' 4th century classic *On the Incarnation* — a short, accessible and powerful reflection on Jesus' identity by a universally respected teacher.

I also encourage you to challenge your pastors to provide solid answers to Jesus' question in their preaching and teaching. In what sense is He both God and man? How is the divine and human united in Christ without confusing those natures or dividing His person? And please don't accept abstract or vague answers. If you want real Christian unity based on the real Person of Jesus Christ, whose real Body is present in the world today through His Church (1 Cor 12:27 and numerous other references), I urge you to seek *real* historical answers to His question. Those who came before us, who suffered and died to proclaim the Jesus Christ of the Apostles, deserve no less an effort from us today.

November 2009

58

The *Holy* Church

In the previous article, I spoke about what (or who) makes the Church "one." Today, I would like to focus on the second adjective that the Nicene Creed applies to the Church: that it is *holy*.

When we think of the concept of "holiness," we tend to imagine a state in which a person can do no wrong and is preserved from evil or sinful behavior. More than that, a holy person only associates with other holy persons. To do otherwise might risk the loss of their "holy" status.

Just this past week someone told me of a group of churches whose location is not widely known. Each community meets in a house and in order to attend, you have to be invited by a member. What is the reason? Simply put, they want to preserve the doctrinal and moral integrity of their community from "disruptive influences" of those who might "drop in." In other words, they maintain their sense of holiness by excluding those who might not be as "pure" as they are.

I bring up this example not to point a finger or to judge, but to suggest that *any* Christian community could fall prey to the same temptation, if we are not vigilant. Most of our churches, while supposedly open to anyone, nevertheless tend to erect barriers at the door: barriers of class and income, barriers of dress and demeanor, and even barriers against those who do not share all our beliefs.

Underlying these invisible but very real restrictions is, I believe, a misunderstanding of what holiness really is.

According to the Scriptures, holiness is less a quality of personal purity than the vocation to belong to God. "I am the LORD who brought you up out of the land of Egypt, to be your God; you shall therefore be holy, for I am holy." (Lev. 11:45) God has chosen His people, rescued them from the bondage of sin and death represented by slavery in Egypt, and now He wants them to be as holy as He is.

That holiness is the condition being set apart from a world that hates and rejects God. It is the calling to live as He made us to live, to be real human beings in His image and likeness, to love our Creator and each other as He loves us. He is our God and we are His people, and that mutual belonging is holiness.

Individual holiness, then, is not measured in the same way as, for instance, the purity of water. When I use holy water to bless people and things, I am not using some kind of "supercharged water"; it's just regular water that has been offered to God to bless His creation. I don't use holy water for any other purpose and I treat it with respect, not because it is somehow purer than tap water, but because it belongs to God for *His* use, and not say, for washing dishes.

What is true for holy water is true for us also. Baptized Christians are not "squeaky clean" human beings who must maintain their spiritual cleanliness by avoiding the unwashed masses who might pollute them. Holiness is not a self-initiated state of purity that we maintain by our own efforts.

On the contrary, Christians are holy in as much as they are ordinary human beings who belong to God for the purpose of showing forth His love for the world every day. Holiness is both God's claim on us as His beloved children, and His challenge for us to live as His people, moment by moment. In this sense, *everyone* is called to be holy, not just an elect and select few.

The holiness of the Church, therefore, has little to do with the individual purity of its members. Rather, *God* is holy and the members of His Body the Church simply participate in that holiness by demonstrating the self-emptying love of God for the world in our daily choices and actions.

The regularity of our church attendance, the correctness of our doctrine, the zeal of our belief, or the strictness of our morality —none of these achievements in any way guarantees our holiness. Indeed, the Church's holiness is tarnished when we uphold our communities as "societies of the pure," because we usurp God's holiness with our own claims to spiritual distinction.

I work at the Salvation Army most days of the week. In my short time there, I have encountered folks who struggle with addictions and abuse, frailty and brokenness of every imaginable kind. On numerous occasions, however, I have wondered how many of these homeless and indigent people would be welcome in a typical Cranbrook church on a given Sunday?

If we hesitate to answer that question honestly, then it's time for us to reevaluate our understanding of holiness. Ultimately, none of us can make a personal claim to be more holy than anyone else. We are all the spiritually marginalized people of God. Those of us who receive the Bread of divine life must reject the temptation to monopolize our claim as invited guests, and simply go about the daily task of showing the rest of the world where the spiritual banquet may be found.

December 2009

The *Catholic* Church

On one level, the Roman Catholic and Eastern Orthodox churches have much in common. Our worship is formal and liturgical, and centers on a weekly celebration of the Eucharist. We are both conscious of the way of life of those who came before us in the faith, and their continuing power to intercede for us as a "cloud of witnesses" in Christ. And we are both hierarchical churches, with bishops, priests and deacons in positions of leadership and authority.

And yet, despite these similarities, our two churches have been divided for over a thousand years, and full communion continues to elude us to this day. Why? After all, aren't the differences between Roman Catholic and Orthodox merely cultural, or simply a question of spiritual style?

The short answer to that question is "no." As similar as the Roman Catholics and Orthodox are in many respects, there exists a fundamental disconnect in our understanding of that third quality ascribed to the Church in the Nicene Creed: that it is "catholic."

Although applied to mean "the Roman Catholic Church," the term "catholic" in fact has a wider meaning, being derived from the Greek word *katholikos* which means effectively, "whole" or "complete."

Here already, though, we run into a problem. What does "whole" or "complete" mean? Does it mean "universal"? Or does it mean "lacking in nothing"? The difference between these two interpretations of "catholic" is one of the key points on which Roman Catholics and Orthodox disagree.

"But what's the big deal?" you may wonder. "'Universal', or 'lacking in nothing.' I don't see any contradiction there!"

To clarify, consider the difference between a bank and a credit union. When you go the local Royal Bank, you are in fact entering to a *branch* of the Royal Bank. The headquarters of the

Royal Bank are elsewhere. The manager of the bank is appointed by the central administration. He or she has authority, but that authority derives from a distant source.

When you go to the Kootenay Savings Credit Union, on the other hand, you are not visiting a branch office. The KSCU is a complete entity constituted and administered by its members. The manager of the credit union derives his authority from a *local* source: the member-elected board.

To speak of the "whole" Royal Bank, you would have to consider all the Royal Bank branches under the authority of the central administration in the entire geographic area where Royal Banks are found. To speak of a "whole" credit union, you would simply point to a local credit union.

What is true of credit unions and banks is loosely true of Roman Catholic and Orthodox churches. Your local Roman Catholic Church is not the "whole" of the Roman Catholic Church; rather, it is a local "branch" whose central administration is in Rome; it is one part of the universal whole.

By contrast, the local Orthodox Church *is* the "whole" Church in that it has everything it needs to be a Church. Ignatius of Antioch, writing in 110 A.D., declared, "Where the bishop is present, there let the congregation gather, just as where Jesus Christ is, there is the Catholic Church." So as long as an Orthodox Church has a Bishop (or a priest appointed to serve on his behalf), and a congregation of baptized Christians, that Church is "whole" and therefore "Catholic."

This distinction between catholic (meaning "universal") and catholic (meaning "lacking in nothing") has real repercussions for the life of the community. The leader of the local Roman Catholic Church (whether a Bishop or priest) is appointed to his position by the central administration in Rome. He has power and authority, but only as it is handed down to him from the Pope.

The leader of the local Orthodox Church is the Bishop, who (in theory at least) is elected by the people of the community and consecrated to his position by at least three other Bishops. The Bishop then may ordain and appoint a priest to serve a given congregation in his stead. In the Orthodox understanding of catholicity, then, authority is grass roots, deriving from the bottom *up*.

An Orthodox Bishop must answer to a council or synod of Bishops, which can discipline and even remove him from power. A hierarch in the Orthodox Church is not the *head* of the Church; that role is reserved for Jesus Christ alone. The Bishop is simply one of the "members of the household of God," (Eph. 2:19) whom the Master has appointed to oversee the running of His household.

As in the analogy of the bank and the credit union, one cannot finally reconcile the Orthodox and Roman Catholic visions of catholicity. Either the local Church is a complete entity, lacking in nothing, or it is one "branch office" of a universal whole. Either the local Bishop is raised to his position by the people of God, or he is appointed to it by Rome.

For Roman Catholic and Orthodox Christians, the basic questions of catholicity must first be answered before full reunion between them is possible: can the Church be complete — *catholic* — without Rome? Can authority exist in the Church without reference to the papal authority?

The rest of us are left with wider questions: what makes the Church complete, whole, *catholic*? For whom do our leaders really get their authority? If we were to choose between the spiritual bank or the spiritual credit union, which would we pick? These are not petty questions. They ultimately concern the Body of Christ, for whom He gave His life, that she might be His spotless Bride.

December 2009

The *Apostolic* Church

In the previous articles, I have tried to address a fundamental question that all Christians face at least once (and probably more than once) in the course of their spiritual lives: *what is the Church?* I have based my answers on the Nicene Creed, that fundamental confession of faith, which applies four descriptors to the Church: that it is *one, holy, catholic* and *apostolic*. Having talked about unity, holiness and catholicity, then, I would like to reflect today on the question of apostolicity and its relevance for us.

Indeed, relevance *is* the very issue at stake when we discuss the question of apostolicity. Many churches today struggle with how to be relevant in a modern and postmodern secular society that seems increasingly indifferent to the Church. They wonder to what extent Christian communities can or should adjust their worship, social programs, and even their teaching to inspire and engage the people of this age, while maintaining a firm grip on the unchanging and ageless truths of Christianity. How do we strike a balance?

The answer varies depending on how we understand apostolicity. According the Eastern Orthodox view, anyway, an apostolic Church is one whose teaching and worship practices are consistent with the experience of the apostles, beginning at their encounter with the risen Jesus Christ on the road to Emmaus. It was on that road that Jesus "interpreted to them in all the scriptures the things concerning himself," (Luke 24:27) before revealing himself to them "in the breaking of the bread." (Luke 24:35)

Because of this seminal experience, the disciples began to proclaim the fundamental Christian proclamation: "The Lord has risen indeed!" (Luke 24:34) In time, they "handed over" their encounter and knowledge of the crucified and risen Lord to the next generation of Christians. As the Apostle Paul tells the Corinthian Church, "For I delivered to you as of first importance *what I also received*, that Christ died for our sins in accordance with the scriptures, that he was buried, that he was raised on the third day in accordance with the scriptures, and that he appeared to Cephas, then to the twelve." (1 Cor. 15:3-5)

According to the Apostle Paul, then, being "apostolic" meant receiving the knowledge that Jesus revealed to His disciples concerning Himself, and faithfully delivered that knowledge to the next generation. This "handing over" involved more than merely conveying information about Jesus to others. Because the disciple knew the Lord in the interpretation of the Scriptures and "the breaking of the bread," the *manner* in which they transmitted that knowledge was also consistent with the way in which they had received it.

Just as the disciples understood Jesus' true identity when Jesus opened their minds to the Scriptures, so too did the Apostles teach those who followed them to begin their worship encounter with Christ by reading and preaching from the Scriptures. And just as the disciples had recognized Jesus when He "took the bread and blessed, and broke it, and gave it to them," (Luke 24:30) so too did the Apostles instruct their communities to receive Christ in the breaking of the bread, which the Apostle Paul understands as the Eucharist, where Christians partake in "the body and blood of the Lord." (1 Cor. 11:27)

What the Apostles taught, that first generation faithfully practiced in their life of faith together. A late first century Church manual known as *Didache* (the text is available online at www.ccel.org) witnesses to the practice of early Christian worship: "On every Lord's Day — His special day — come together, and break bread and give thanks, first confessing your sins so that your sacrifice may be pure." The document also gives specific instructions on how the Eucharist is to be offered and prayed over during the service...

From the beginning, then, an apostolic Church was a community that faithfully received and transmitted the knowledge of the crucified and risen Christ in a manner consistent with that of the disciples who met Jesus on the road to Emmaus.

This "handing over" was not just slavish imitation or the mere preservation of dead rituals and doctrines. It is clear from the history of the Church that each succeeding generation of Christians appropriated and personalized the faith they received from the Apostles, making it unique and alive in their own time and place. Despite these developments, however, the apostolic Church maintained the scriptural and Eucharistic elements that the Apostles themselves would have recognized in their own teachings and practices.

What does this mean for us? I began this article by saying that many Christian communities today are seeking to be relevant to our secular society by adjusting worship styles, methods of ministry and even doctrinal teaching to suit their congregations. The problem with this approach, I would argue, is that in pursuing ever more current ways of expressing the faith, churches run the risk of forsaking their apostolic vocation.

In seeking greater relevance through worldly means (MTV-style music, multimedia presentations, dumbed-down preaching, etc.), Christian communities are in danger of losing the only relevance they have ever really possessed in this world: their identity as the faithful bearers of the original apostolic encounter with the crucified and risen Christ, who is "the same yesterday and today and forever." (Heb. 13:8)

Adapting to the challenge of the modern world is indeed crucial to the mission of the Church. More essential to the *nature* of the Church, however, is its call to be apostolic, to hold fast that which has been delivered to us by the Apostles. Abandoning this fundamental vocation to pursue adaptation, compromise and innovation is simply too high a price to pay to fill a church building on a Sunday morning. After all, as Jesus Himself says, "What does

it profit a man to gain the world and forfeit his soul?" (Mark 8:36)
December 2009

There's Something About Mary

Mary, the mother of Jesus, is not a prominent presence in the New Testament. We read of her encounter with the Archangel Gabriel, in which she accepts her role as the one who will give birth to the Son of God with the famous statement, "Behold, I am the handmaid of the Lord; let it be to me according to your word." (Luke 1:38) She sings an ode to God called the *Magnificat*. (Luke 1:46-55) Later, she encourages her son to perform his first miracle at the wedding in Cana of Galilee. She appears sporadically during Jesus' ministry, and is present at the Cross. Other than that, however, the Bible has little to say about Mary.

For many, such scriptural silence is proof that Mary was little more than a human vessel for the divine initiative. Though a faithful disciple of Christ, she does not warrant the fuss that Orthodox and Roman Catholics have made about her over the centuries.

I do not intend to offer a comprehensive defence of the Orthodox Christian veneration of Mary in this article. Rather, I would invite you to reconsider Mary's role in the unfolding of God's revelation by asking two basic questions.

Firstly, *what does it mean to say that Mary was Jesus' mother?* Scholars of the ancient world tell us that in the time of Jesus, mothers were entirely responsible for the raising of children at least until the age of five. Those first five years of life are now recognized to be crucial in the development of a child's personality.

The Bible tells us that Jesus "grew and became strong, filled with wisdom; and the favor of God was upon him." (Luke 2:40) If Jesus was indeed like us in every respect, his growth and development would certainly not have been self-generated and self-guided. Like all children of his time, his mother would have been responsible for raising, guiding, teaching and nurturing him. Although the Bible says little of Jesus' early years, it hardly needs to spell out the uncountable personal sacrifices Mary would have made for her child during that time. If we downplay the importance of her role, what are we saying about the place of mothers in the development of the spiritual life of their children?

The second question to ask as we consider the relevance of Mary to Christian faith is, *what does it mean to give birth to God in the flesh?* The fundamental confession of the Christian faith is that Jesus is fully God and fully man. Mary, then, gave birth to one who was both a man and *at the same time* "God with us." This quite literally makes Mary the mother of the man Jesus *and* "the Mother of God," because the One whom she bore was God in the flesh. Indeed, this is the title by which Orthodox Christians refer to Mary — Theotokos, which is Greek for "Mother of God." It seems paradoxical, but the logic is inevitable.

To call Mary "the Mother of God" does not imply that she stands apart as a different class of human being. According to Orthodox Church teaching anyway, Mary was born as a fallen human being, just like the rest of us. Her life was not sinless, and she died just as we do (though we would assert that she was raised from the dead and taken into heaven, like Enoch and the prophet Elijah). Extraordinary as her life and role was, Mary stands firmly as an ordinary member of the human race.

That being said, it does not follow that anyone could have taken Mary's place in the unfolding of God's plan of salvation. Not only did she have to be a woman in order to give birth, her calling to be Theotokos also meant an exceptional level of *spiritual* preparedness, as well as a unique and exclusive calling to holiness.

Consider again her response to the Archangel Gabriel: "Behold, I am the handmaid of the Lord; let it be to me according to your word." How many of the fourteen-year-old girls you know could have answered in this way? Would they not be more likely to dismiss, deny, or simply react out of fear? Mary's words are concise, but they speak volumes about the state of her soul and the attitude of her heart, which was the product of years of faithfulness and submission to God. Her answer to the Archangel was nothing less than bold, heroic, and ultimately, a model of Christian discipleship and obedience.

Being "the Mother of God" also meant that Mary was specially set aside for God's purposes, i.e. holy. This is why *every* Christian teacher until the Reformation (Luther, Zwingli and Wesley included) universally asserted that Mary that she was not only a virgin before bearing Christ, but remained one afterwards and for the rest of her life, and that Jesus' 'siblings' were either cousins or Joseph's children by a former marriage.

We can perhaps see their reasoning. If Mary is indeed "the Mother of God," then her conception and birth-giving was a unique event, consecrating her womb as a temple exclusive to God. If, however, Mary was just another Jewish housewife, the mother of Joseph's kids, and Jesus was just one more child in her brood, what does that say about the holiness of God and the uniqueness of Jesus' conception as the Son of God?

It seems to me that such questions are worth asking about Mary. If we honour Abraham, Isaac and Jacob, Moses and David and Solomon, who were ultimately prophets proclaiming God's Word, surely we can give some consideration to the one who was not only obedient to God's Word, but bore that "Word made flesh" in her womb?

September 2009

Three Misconceptions About Heaven And Hell

The question of heaven and hell provides Christian teachers with some of our most troublesome moments. After all, it is difficult to promote and defend the idea that at some point, God will reward all the good little boys and girls by giving them clouds in the air, angels' wings and harps, while sending the 'sinners' into a big pit, where demons with pitchforks gleefully await, ready to deal out eternal torments.

Caricatured as I have made it, my sketch reflects to large extent the popular notion of how Christians view the last judgement and the afterlife. Indeed, I often deal with Christians who, though not consciously touting literal wings and harps or devils with red-hot pitchforks, are nevertheless labouring under a number of misconceptions of a genuine scriptural Christian understanding of the meaning of heaven and hell. I would therefore like to offer some responses to three common misconceptions concerning the afterlife.

1. Heaven and hell are physical places. Since its inception in the 14th century, Dante's *Divine Comedy* has dominated our western imaginative view of heaven and hell. Reasonable Christians, however, know that hell is not really a vast conical pit descending to the centre of the earth; nor is purgatory a mountain, nor heaven a series of spheres expanding into the heavens. No matter how compelling Dante's imaginative poetic vision may have been, he never intended it to constitute a theology or doctrine.

Neither hell nor heaven are places that can be reached by any physical means. Rather, they are the spiritual conditions of either rejecting the Presence of God or embracing it. The rejection of God's Presence is the defining quality of hell. As Milton says of that archetypal rebel Satan, "... for within him Hell / He brings, and round about him, nor from Hell / One step no more than from himself can fly / By change of place..." Neither hell nor heaven are geographic locales; they are attitudes. Hell is the eternal refusal of the invitation to be with God, and heaven is the eternal delight in His Presence.

2. Heaven is nearness to God, while hell is separation from Him. In fact, through His death, Christ "descended into the lower parts of the earth" (Eph. 4:9) so that He might fill all things with Himself. (Eph. 1:23) As the Psalmist says, "Whither shall I go from Your Spirit? Or whither shall I flee from Your presence? If I ascend to heaven, You are there! If I make my bed in Sheol, You are there!" (Ps. 139:7-8)

In the age to come, therefore, God will come to be everywhere and fill all things: "And I saw the holy city, new Jerusalem, coming down out of heaven from God, prepared as a bride adorned for her husband; and I heard a loud voice from the throne saying, "Behold, the dwelling of God is with men. He will dwell with them, and they shall be his people, and God himself will be with them." (Rev. 21:2-3)

In the Eastern Orthodox understanding, the new world will be not be a "second creation," since God resolved never to destroy His creation after the Flood (Gen. 8:21-22). Rather, the new world will be *this* world — purified and cleansed by the fire of suffering (see 2 Peter 3:10), until it is finally transformed and transfigured into the paradise for which it was originally created, where God can return to dwell with His people.

In this view, hell will simply be the way in which those who reject and hate God will experience a new world where He cannot be evaded, while heaven will be the *same* experience from the point of view of those who love Him. As Saint Isaac of Syria says, "Those who find themselves in Gehenna [that is, hell] will be chastised with the scourge of love. How cruel and bitter this torment of love will be! For those who understand that they have sinned against love undergo greater sufferings than those produced of the most fearful tortures. The sorrow which takes hold of the heart which has sinned against love is more piercing than any other pain. It is not right to say that sinners in hell are deprived of the love of God. ... But love acts in two different ways, as suffering in the reproved, and as joy in the blessed."

3. The torments of hell are external. This perceived teaching is perhaps the greatest difficulty that many have with the notion of hell. How could a loving God actively torture people by some perverse means? How could a loving God takes delight in the punishment and pain of His people? The answer is, God neither torments us, nor takes delight in our punishment. If hell is the experience of God's loving Presence by those who reject Him, then the torment and punishment is entirely self-inflicted. God does not send anyone to hell; *we* make hell when we turn away from Him. As Milton's Satan say, "Me miserable! Which way shall I fly / Infinite wrath, and infinite despair? / Which way I fly is Hell; myself am Hell..."

To put it simply: God loves us and has come to be with us in Christ. For now, the full impact of His coming is still unfolding, but in time it will stand fully revealed and manifest to all humanity. "For now we see in a mirror dimly, but then face to face. Now I know in part; then I shall understand fully, even as I have been fully understood." (1 Cor. 13:12) In the end, everything will come down to the same love of God, a love we can know either as good news indeed and joy forever, or the inescapable realization of our worst nightmare. How we know that love—as heaven or as hell—is entirely up to us.

March 2009

Baptizing the Culture

A Co-Suffering Culture

Violence Unveiled

I am in the process of reading a fascinating (if difficult) book recommended to me by one of my parishioners entitled *Violence Unveiled*. The author, Gil Bailie, is a Christian anthropologist who explores the phenomenon of violence in modern society through the lens of the Gospel.

Bailie uses the work of French philosopher Rene Girard to suggest that the increasing violence of today's world is the result of a breakdown between "sacred" and "profane" forms of violence, a breakdown that began with the coming of Christ, His death and resurrection.

Bailie's argument is complex, but it goes something as follows. Society has always struggled with destructive violence. Before Christianity, societies dealt with this violence by turning their violent impulses on a scapegoat—a person or a marginalized group with obvious differences from themselves.

By elevating violence against the scapegoat to the level of religious mythology, societies were able to use "good" violence against the scapegoat to unite their peoples and bring an end to the "bad" violence that threatened to tear them apart. As long as everyone within that society continued to believe the mythology, they would remain united in their common enmity against the scapegoat, as opposed to being torn apart by internal conflicts.

For this system to work, however, members of a society had to rid themselves of one key quality: pity. For as long as they could manage to regard their victims without pity, they could continue to justify their violence as a necessary part of a divine mythology of redemption and salvation.

The crucifixion of Jesus was supposed to be one more instance of this mechanism, which tries to combat "bad" violence with "good" violence. As Caiaphas, the high priest in the Gospel of John says, "it is expedient for you that one man should die for the people, and that the whole nation should not perish." (John 11:50)

The Gospel, however, threw a spanner into the works, because in this case the victim of Jewish "sacred" violence — Jesus — is proclaimed as the king and conqueror of death. In the words of the Apostle Paul, the One who was humbled even to death has been exalted and given "the name which is above every name, that at the name of Jesus every knee should bow, in heaven and on earth and under the earth, and every tongue confess that Jesus Christ is Lord, to the glory of God the Father." (Phil. 2:9-11)

The Gospel event has had profound implications on subsequent history, according to Bailie. Since then, societies that have encountered and fallen under the influence of the crucifixion and resurrection of Jesus can no longer rid themselves of pity for their scapegoats — at least not for very long.

The Gospel of Jesus Christ has awakened in human society a sense of *com*-passion for *all* victims, and as a result, we can no longer pretend that our scapegoats are just an abstract part of the religious myths that justify our "good" acts of violence as an antidote for violence that would tear us apart.

Of course, so-called "Christian" societies since the Gospel have frequently engaged in scapegoating violence: the persecution of Jews throughout Western European history, culminating in the Holocaust, is just one of many instances.

Bailie's point, though, is that although modern societies still try to cure destructive violence with "sacred" violence, the Gospel has ensured that those of us under its influence can no longer make the cure "stick." We inevitably "wake up" tormented by the feeling that we have somehow crucified Jesus all over again.

And Bailie's central point is that, increasingly, the traditional cure for destructive violence in the world is becoming less and less effective. We are less and less able to distinguish between violence that destroys and violence that unites, because the Gospel has completely overthrown our ability to believe in the curative power of violent acts, no matter how exalted the terms in which they are justified: the so-called "War against Terror" is just one example.

Although I haven't gotten there yet, Bailie is already implying a Christian response to this conundrum. While the Passion may be responsible for our collective inability to remain pitiless towards our scapegoats, it also offers us a way beyond the whole system that makes scapegoats necessary in the first place.

Rather than using sacred violence to try and cure destructive violence in society, the Gospel presents an alternative: a culture of co-suffering. This way of life rests on the proclamation that God is the One who suffers with all of us. As creatures made in God's image and likeness, therefore, our very human identity depends on a commitment to suffer daily with each other.

The God who Suffers

To begin, we need to state explicitly what we believe about the Jesus of whom we are speaking. If we are indeed created in God's image and likeness, then His identity shapes who we are, which in turn affects how we behave towards each other. While not an end in and of themselves, beliefs are foundational to everything we do.

If we are to build a culture of co-suffering, then, we must first clearly say that Jesus – and thus, God – is none other the One who *suffers with* us. In past articles, I have defined suffering as being powerless over forces beyond our control. Jesus suffered in that He was subject to time constraints, gravity, hunger and thirst, ignorance of the future, and ultimately, death on the Cross. That the eternal God who is beyond suffering, who cannot be subject to anything, would reveal Himself in this way is the central Mystery of the Christian faith. We don't try to explain the spiritual mechanics – that's why it's called a "mystery" – but the declaration is central to our belief and therefore, our life of faith.

According to the Eastern Orthodox teaching, Jesus did not suffer so that we don't have to. Like Adam, we squandered the good life God has given us, frittering away our humanity and digging ourselves into a debt of inhumanity against ourselves, and each other. In this state of rebellion, we experience God's eternal love as a fire of divine wrath that will consume and destroy us unless our humanity is restored.

In this understanding, Jesus' sacrifice is not a ransom payment to the devil, as if God should reward the evil one who instigated our fall in the first place. Neither is Jesus' sacrifice to His Father since, as Gregory the Theologian puts it, "it was not by [the Father] that we were being oppressed. And ... on what principle did the Blood of His only-begotten Son delight the Father, who would not receive even Isaac, when he was being sacrificed by his father, but changed the sacrifice by putting a ram in the place of the human victim?"

Rather than a legal payoff to God or the devil, Jesus' sacrifice was a payment made *to our fallen condition*. We mortgaged our human worth to pay for the false thrills of sin. In His life and death on the Cross, Jesus has paid off that debt, restoring us to our true worth by filling up what we lost from the treasury of His full and perfect humanity.

Jesus suffered, then, not merely to erase suffering, but to teach us what it means to be truly human. And being truly human is fundamentally about accepting that we are powerless creatures, subject to forces beyond our control.

Why is this important? Because ending history's cycle of violence and building a new culture means abandoning all attempts to define ourselves through the use and abuse of power, a process that always uses violence to achieve its selfish ends. Instead, we are called to embrace a new identity of shared personal powerlessness that unites us to each other. And that identity is rooted ultimately in the One who became powerless for us and who leads us through suffering, death, and into a resurrected life beyond.

Suffering as Personal Powerlessness

Co-suffering as a way of life may sound rather gloomy, but only if you think of suffering as meaning nothing more than pain. In reality, suffering has a larger denotation. It is being subject to things beyond our control.

Understood in this sense, suffering is integral part of being human, because as human beings, we are subject to (at the very least) the four dimensions of time and space. I could be enjoying a bowl of ice cream on a sunny day, with not a care in the world, and still be suffering, simply because even when I am blissfully happy, I cannot prevent the clock from ticking or the world from turning.

Suffering, then, is not just about pain or misery. It is a condition of our existence. But it is not a condition that we like very much. Indeed, it might be said that the whole of the western secular enterprise rests on a belief that we can and should escape from suffering through human ingenuity.

What is the impetus for modern science and technology except the impulse to free us from nature's control through greater knowledge? What is the sign of a healthy economy but "growth," by which we mean the increased power of consumers over their spending limits? What drives politics except the acquisition of power to control the destinies of nations? What motivates social, religious, and others trends but our endless quest for self-determination?

Our society's most precious if unspoken ideal is that if we can just learn enough, get rich enough, healthy enough, powerful enough, or just happy enough, then all poverty and suffering will cease. We will finally be free. We may even reach the point where we do not need to die…

I am not here to argue with those who passionately uphold this belief. I *will* say that the arrogant compulsion of scientists and technocrats to discover at all costs, of market economies to grow and prosper at all costs, and of the individuals and nations to "get happy" at the cost of other individuals and nations, are even now tearing our world apart. Glorious as the secular humanist vision may be, I am not sure the world will survive long enough to see it fulfilled…

80

A culture of co-suffering offers a radical alternative. It begins with a conscious acceptance that suffering is an inescapable fact of life and that there will always be realities beyond our control.

This decision—which 12-Step addicts call "an admission of powerlessness"—is a profound act that initiates a genuine faith in God and fundamentally reorients the ways in which we choose to live our lives.

Consider how our spending choices might change if we collectively refused to buy into the commercial deceit that this or that product will enable us to escape the unsatisfactory lives we now live and attain a "better" destiny. We might well see the end of growth based market economies and the beginning of something else. What else, you might wonder? How about a steady state economy that organizes its activities based on sustainability and ecological responsibility?

Consider what might happen if science and technology were no longer driven by the impulse to improve on the human race, regardless of the expense. We might well see a considerable slowing of our breakneck development in many fields, but really, would that be such a tragedy? If Bach composed and Michelangelo painted in a society afflicted with the plague, without electricity and running water, would it be so terrible if we were deprived of yet another version of the iPad?

These are just two implications of the choice to accept personal powerlessness. Rather than asking ourselves, "What else is there to get or become?" and then pursuing our answers at the expense of others and our world as a whole, a culture of co-suffering challenges us to pray what you might know as the "Serenity Prayer": *God, grant me the serenity to accept the things I cannot change, the courage to change the things I can, and the wisdom to know the difference.*

On the basis of this personal commitment, we can take the next step in implementing a truly compassionate culture.

Mutual Weakness

I wish today's Christian communities could offer living examples of co-suffering cultures. Sadly, most do not. Despite the calling of the Gospel, we Christians have often chosen to take the opposite tack and define ourselves in enmity with others. The Koran-burning in Gainesville and the deadly counter-protests in Kabul are an example of what happens when this latent tendency is taken to its logical extreme.

Given that we contemporary Christians have a limited understanding of the challenge of our own Gospel, fresh insight must come from unexpected places. Where better to look for a co-suffering culture, then, but among those who are more acutely aware of their own powerlessness, and who seek freedom by sharing a common struggle? I am speaking here, of course, of recovering addicts in the 12-Step program.

I have often spoken of the 12 Steps, which are rooted in the Gospel and present the heart of Christianity in ways that are practical and accessible, not just for addicts, but for anyone seeking spiritual clarity. I will add here that the 12-Step program is not a substitute for historic Christianity, but a prophetic reminder — when we are tempted to forget — of the Gospel's inner meaning. Similarly, 12-Step recovery groups are not Church substitutes, but offer a vision for the conduct of authentic Christian community.

Let's consider specifically one of the fundamental rules of every 12-Step meeting: 'no cross-talk.' In 12-Step lingo, 'cross-talk' is defined as directly addressing advice, comments or questions to someone else in the group. In the 12-Step context, the absence of cross-talk is essential so that members can feel safe to share freely and completely, without risking judgement, criticism or unwanted attention.

At a deeper level, the 'no cross-talk' rule has a spiritual purpose: it ensures that members are not tempted to exert power over others with their words. Each person can only share from his or her own human experience without prescribing how another should behave. As a result, the only authority permitted in the meeting is that of the 'Higher Power' of God, while everyone else speaks simply as one of His servants.

We can perhaps see how the 'no cross-talk' rule might speak to communities well beyond the 12-Step program, beginning with churches. Imagine a Church community where no one offers advice, platitudes, judgments or criticisms. Imagine Church leaders whose authority is rooted only in service and example.

Now imagine the 'no cross talk' rule applied to all human communities, so that members no longer seek to exert power over each other legally, financially, socially, religiously or sexually, but instead relate to each other simply on the basis of their shared human experience. Imagine governments whose rule rests on their service to their people, rather than on the drive to control them. Imagine nations that no longer seek to pursue their ideological or economic interests at the expense of other nations...

None of these are new ideals; they exist already, enshrined in many of our Church doctrines and social constitutions, and they all derive ultimately from the New Testament itself. The 'no cross talk' rule acts simply as a lens to focus us on those Gospel elements that are most essential and yet most easily forgotten.

As we strive to build a Gospel culture, however, we will encounter those who won't abide by the 'no cross talk' rule. They insist on asserting their power over others through violence, or try to cure violence by violent means. How do we respond?

In my estimation, pacifism is not the answer. When someone invades my home and threatens my family, I am obligated to respond, violently if necessary. If a government starts murdering its people, the international community must intervene, violently if necessary. The difference lies in our attitude. Do we justify our violence using quasi-sacred words like 'rights' and 'freedom' and 'democracy'? Do we continue trying to invest our violent actions with moral legitimacy? Do we depict Qaddafi and his supporters as monsters so that our own bombings and killings can shine with a self-righteous light?

The culture of co-suffering calls us to a different attitude. If we must shoot and bomb, we have to do so in full knowledge that we are not just 'neutralizing' tanks and anti-aircraft guns, but killing men, making widows of their wives, and orphans of their children. We must weep for those whom we have killed, and our direct role in destroying the lives of their families. Finally, our violence must lead us repent of the rivalries and power struggles in our own lives, and turn towards the One who told His disciples, "Put your sword back into its place; for all who take the sword will perish by the sword." (Matt 26:52)

In short, the path to a co-suffering culture is neither easy nor clear cut. It is not simply a matter of more legislation or better education or more effective social or evangelical programs. Rather, it begins in each and every human heart. With time and patience, with steps forward and steps backward, people transformed into the image and likeness of the Suffering God can begin to build communities based on their shared identity in Him, so that slowly, heart by heart and community by community, across regional, national and international boundaries, a new world of compassion, peace and joy may be born.

February-April 2011

Corner Gas and the Need to Belong

My favourite TV show of all time is *Corner Gas*, that much beloved Canadian sitcom that entertained us for six seasons with the ordinary yet hilarious lives of the residents of Dog River, Sasketchewan. No matter how many time I watch the episodes (I have lost count by now), I am always delighted at the show's witty dialogue, uproarious situations, and eccentric characters. There's something comforting about *Corner Gas*, like going back to your parent's home after years of being away, and finding that your old room is just as you left it.

Perhaps because theology is my stock in trade, I am always looking for a spiritual source for my joy and satisfaction in the details of earthly life. My pleasure in *Corner Gas* is no different. What is it about the lives of these normal people in a small Sasketchewan town that I find so... beautiful? What makes that ordinariness so wonderful?

A piece of dialogue from the first season of the show offers some insight. In the introductory scene, one of the main characters, Wanda Dollard, is sitting at the counter of the gas station where she works. Because this is a small town in the middle of nowhere, she doesn't have much to do, and so she is reading, not a magazine, but a textbook.

A customer enters and the following dialogue takes place:

Customer: What's that, quantum physics?

Wanda: Yeah, I've always been fascinated that light could be a particle and a wave. I was gonna study it in college, but then I got interested in biochemistry. And then on a whim settled on liguistics with a minor in comparative religion.

Customer: Wow, how'd you end up in a place like this?

Wanda Dollard: The last girl quit, can you believe it?

While some of the humour of this exchange is lost without the nuance that good actors can deliver, the inner irony of the joke is evident in the writing. Of all the career heights Wanda could scale, the work she most wants to be doing is that of a CSR at a rather dull and dingy gas station in a town of a 100 odd people in the middle of the prairies.

Dog River is a place in which nothing happens. It's boring and dull. No one in the outside world knows or cares all that much about it. It is not the centre of anything. And yet, for all that, the people of Dog River are not only content to live there, they wouldn't live anywhere else! What makes the show truly funny with repeated viewings is in the characters' irrepressible conviction that this nothing little town is really the best of all possible worlds.

Of course, Dog River is an idealized vision that finds predecessors in other fictional Canadian small towns, such as Leacock's Mariposa in *Sunshine Sketches of a Little Town*. At the heart of the vision, though, lies a universal human need that far exceeds the need to discover, acquire, achieve or succeed: the need to belong.

Jean Vanier, the founder of L'Arche, once said that the human need to belong is greater than the need to be loved. It's a bold claim, but one that bears itself out in observation. Consider how many battered spouses endure their marriages simply because they cannot imagine belonging anywhere else. Consider how many young people join gangs or popular groups, not because they are well treated, but because they feel at home in those groups.

In fact, the need to belong is ultimately spiritual in nature. Our inner drive to find our own versions of Dog River — places, relationships, communities in which we can find total acceptance and peace — derive from a deeper desire to find our hearts' true home in God Himself. St. Augustine famously said, "Almighty God, you have made us for Yourself, and our hearts are restless till they find their rest in You."

When this yearning for our home in God is not met, we seek all kinds of substitutes. We may endure abusive relationships and gravitate towards cults and sects. Many of us are already inclined to find solace in virtual pseudo-communities like Facebook. Or we may strive through social and political action to realize the Dog River ideal of belonging in our own neighbourhoods and towns. But unless we find the real Source of our yearning for home in our Creator, our fundamental loneliness and restlessness will continue to consume us.

The Gospel offers us the way back to true belonging. The life, death and resurrection of Jesus Christ was not merely an exercise in legal-spiritual debt management. More than just dying in our stead, Jesus died in our place—that is, He died just as we do —so that He could bring us back home to God. With the Cross and the Resurrection, we are no longer far from God, restlessly seeking our belonging in Him. Rather, He has put His Kingdom within us (Luke 17:21) and single-handedly brought us back to where we belong in His Presence.

As we continue to bask in the light of the Easter season, then, the Gospel challenges us to give up our restless search for belonging in the many substitutes that cannot and do not satisfy, and to realize that in Christ, we truly belong, which means simply that in Him, we are loved, accepted, embraced without reservation. In Him, we are at home, once and for all. Our only task—the task for the rest of our lifetimes—is to accept the fact and live accordingly.

April 2011

House, M.D. and the Power of the Formula

One of the ways in which my wife and I unwind in the evenings is to watch TV shows on DVD. An enduring favourite is *House, M.D.*, a medical procedural starring Hugh Laurie as Dr. Gregory House, a misanthropic genius who leads a team of diagnosticians to detect the causes and cures of mysterious ailments.

Other than the characters themselves (and particularly House himself), what I most enjoy about the show is its ongoing formula. Each episode usually begins with a crisis that leads to someone collapsing. Following the introductory credits, House and his team take on the case and for about twenty minutes of screen time, they explore false leads and hit two or three dead end diagnoses, while grappling with various personal issues.

Then comes the moment when some offhand comment leads House to get that wide-eyed faraway look of his, mutter something cryptic, and walk out of the room without explanation. That's how you know he's solved the case, either happily (a curable disease) or tragically (something incurable).

And that's the show, 42 minutes at a time, disease after disease, for seven seasons and counting. Some episodes have broken the mould, but I haven't enjoyed them as much. *House* works best when it sticks to the formula.

Perhaps you have similar feelings about your own favourite TV show. Or perhaps you love to read an author whose books follow a familiar pattern. Whatever the case may be, I am sure there are some aspects of your life that follow a formula—a set routine within which you feel comfortable and happy.

Formula is essential to a healthy human life. We seem to need it from the beginning. Babies need a regular bedtime ritual to learn how to sleep well by themselves. Children want the same story read to them every day for weeks at a time...

Case in point: recently, we took our children to see the most recent Narnia movie. While the older kids enjoyed it, my four-year-old was restless and even bored. When we buy *The Voyage of the Dawn Treader* on DVD, however, you can bet he will watch and rewatch the movie for days at a time, until he can quote it by heart.

This seems to defy logic. You might think novelty would be more engaging and exciting, whereas repetition would get dull and boring. Paradoxically, it is not so, at least for those who are experiencing life for the first time. Children seem to need time and repetition to explore a given experience more thoroughly and deeply. It needs to become a formula before they can fully understand it.

This tendency in children, who tend to be more sensitive to the multiple dimensions of life, offers a lesson for us adults. After all, isn't novelty the constant dilemma of many churches? How many communities ask themselves how can the services, the sermon and the music be contemporized so that young people might want to keep coming to church even after Dad and Mum stop forcing them?

The problem, as is almost always the case, lies with the assumptions underlying the question. Those seeking relevancy assume that if you give people something new to experience on regular basis, their interest will be captured and held. Then the only problem is how to keep it fresh, week by week.

Louder music, flags and banners, song-and-dance routines, slick videos, Holy Spirit pyrotechnics, cutesy kiddy set pieces, media stunts — these innovations are often just attempts to attract attention through novelty. And as time goes on, communities must play for this gamble with ever higher stakes, as their church attendance becomes dependent on the innovativeness of this Sunday's episode...

What is lost in this cycle? Depth. A friend of mine recently shared that he cannot pray in a church until he has learned what is coming next in the service. Why? Because full engagement requires sustained attention, and sustained attention requires that a person not be on-guard, jittery or anxious, as we often are when placed in novel situations. Worship based on novelty will produce excitement and crowds, but not prayerfulness, simply because people will not be able to settle down enough to focus on prayer.

One might assume that if we take away the novelties, people will become bored and end up going through the motions of "dead religion." I am here to tell you that it simply isn't so. In the worship of my own church community (which is about as far from novelty as you can get), I have seen children, youth and adult get more engaged the longer they attend, not less. As their familiarity with the service increases, they understand more and are able to participate more in the ways available to them. They know what's coming next, so they can easily find a way to enter into what's happening.

For millennia, human beings have needed formula. It's the secret of our most enduring art; it lies at the root of our psychology; it forms the basis of our worship. After all, if we have always been human, God has always been God. As the Apostle writing to the Hebrews says, "Jesus Christ is the same, yesterday, today and forever." If we haven't changed and God hasn't changed, is there really a better formula to meeting Him than the one used since the beginning by those who have come before us?

January 2011

The Dark Christ

A few nights ago, I watched for the second time Christopher Nolan's *The Dark Knight*. I had seen the movie in the theatre and was impressed, but the second viewing sealed it for me. *The Dark Knight* now stands on my list of all-time great films, with movies such as *Star Wars* (the original trilogy) and *The Shawshank Redemption*.

This seems like an odd statement to make about a film based on a cartoon superhero. However, *The Dark Knight* is indeed a great film precisely because it transcends the requirements and expectations of the superhero genre in order to explore a thematic realm that I can only describe as profoundly spiritual.

Superhero stories have always possessed the potential to retell spiritual stories. The best of them (the first *Superman* movie, for example, or *Spiderman 2*) clearly reveal the spiritual symbolism implicit in the superhero genre as a whole — that transcendent beings exist to save us from evil forces that seek to destroy the world.

The Dark Knight goes one step further. Not merely content to retell the metaphor of superhero-as-saviour, Nolan's film explores with unnerving clarity the spiritual realities that underpin our entire civilization, realities on which we depend for our very survival — whether we acknowledge that dependence or not.

Although this article is not intended as a movie review, some recap is necessary. Gotham city is under threat once more, this time from the Joker, a psychotic maniac backed by a small army of equally psychotic thugs. The Joker appeared in the first *Batman* movie, played by Jack Nicholson as a theatrical showman whose diabolical purposes, though twisted, are driven by base greed and the need for revenge.

Nolan's version of the Joker is nothing like the Nicholson character. Brilliantly performed by the late Heath Ledger, the Joker in *The Dark Knight* has no rational purpose. "Do I look like a man with a plan?" he asks at one point. The answer is a resounding no. As Bruce Wayne's butler Alfred remarks early on, "Some men just like to watch the world burn." The Joker is just that: an irrational force of chaos and destruction. He is not motivated by greed, revenge or any other material consideration. He exists simply to ruin that which is good, to bring to nothing our best laid plans, to disorder the order of the world.

Watching the film with Christian eyes, I could not help but recall Saint Paul's words to the Romans: "I do not do the good I want, but the evil I do not want is what I do." (Romans 7:18-19) As a diabolical agent seeking to subvert and sabotage humanity's best intentions, the Joker embodies a fundamental demonic spiritual force lurking in the human heart, whose only purpose is to tear down, destroy and watch the world burn.

Against this satanic force, the film pits Harvey Dent, Gotham's District Attorney. Dent is described as a 'white knight': a noble man with the best will and intentions. Tirelessly crusading for justice, he symbolizes all of Gotham's hopes, which are the hopes of every civilization: that law and order and peace are possible and will prevail. However, when personal tragedy (instigated by the Joker) befalls him, Dent proves as fallible as anyone else, degenerating into the bitter and twisted Two-Face.

The film's point seems clear: human civilization cannot survive on the strength of its best intentions and noble efforts. Humanism—the belief in humanity's innate will to accomplish good—is not enough. Even at its best, the human race will always sabotage itself, because it is subject to the destructive force of the Joker. Our lament will always echo Saint Paul: "I can will what is right, but I cannot do it."

In the end, Harvey Dent's reputation is preserved, but only through a public cover-up to bolster the faith and hope of the people of Gotham. Real salvation, however, lies elsewhere, in the person of Batman himself.

Here, in my opinion, is where the film really soars: Batman willingly agrees to be blamed for Harvey Dent's crimes, and by implication, the crimes of all Gotham. In the closing scene he declares, "You'll hunt me. You'll condemn me, set the dogs on me, because it's what needs to happen..." Commissioner Gordon, who witnesses this self-sacrifice, explains that Batman must be hunted because "he can take it. Because he's not our hero. He's a silent guardian, a watchful protector, a dark knight."

Once again, my Christian eyes and ears could not help but return to Christ, who was blamed for the sins of Israel and killed as a criminal. Nor could I help but recall how the Psalmist prophesied that sacrificial death: "Dogs are round about me; a company of evildoers encircle me; they have pierced my hands and feet..." (Psalm 22:16)

Indeed, by offering himself as a sacrifice, Batman becomes what literary scholars call a "Christ figure" — someone who symbolically reenacts the life and death of Christ. In this, Batman stands beside many such characters in film and fiction. Luke Skywalker is a Christ figure, and in the most brilliant and crucial twist of the *Star Wars* saga, Dark Vader becomes one too. *Shawshank's* Andy Dufresne also follows a Christ-like path — an innocent victim who enters into the darkness of a prison and redeems its inmates.

The Dark Knight is worth watching, not just because it is well-made, but for its spiritual insight. Films such as these demonstrate that while our society rejects and denies Christianity, it cannot help but replay the Greatest Story Ever Told in the symbols and metaphors of its popular culture. Like the citizens of Gotham, who need Batman in order to survive, but can't admit to that need, our civilization needs a Jesus Christ; it needs someone who can 'take' everything — all our weaknesses, our failures, our sins — who is willing to be our 'Dark Knight' so that hope and peace can prevail in the city of this world.

August 2009

Some Thoughts on Avatar

Before I begin, let me be clear that I am not a movie critic and the following article is not a review of James Cameron's blockbuster sci-epic *Avatar.* Having seen the movie recently, having noted its almost 'titanic' popularity, I thought it might be worthwhile to offer a reflection on the spiritual themes that stand at the centre of the film. A warning, though: spoilers will follow. Let the reader beware!

As a visual experience, *Avatar* was really a treat. Combining the very best in CGI with tasteful and awesome 3-D and motion capture technologies, Cameron creates a world called Pandora and a race called the Na'vi that are rich and varied and strangely beautiful. Though the story is familiar—a recycled blend of *Dances with Wolves* and *Pocahontas*—as a piece of pure entertainment point of view, *Avatar* is well worth whatever you might pay to see a movie in the theatre these days.

My concern lies with the *spiritual* vision beneath *Avatar*'s visual finery. Simply, Cameron sets up two understandings of the world and pits them, one against the other, what is known as a dialectic: an either/or situation between which we must choose. The choice, I would suggest, is a false one, but I am getting ahead of myself...

On one hand, *Avatar* presents a materialistic view of the human race. It seems that in the future, human beings will degenerate into energy-starved marauders whose sole purpose is to find new worlds and strip them of the resources to keep their economy afloat (in the case of Pandora, it is a mineral called Unobtanium).

In this dystopia, humanity is divided between rationalistic scientists who investigate Pandora, and soldiers who provide the necessary muscle to take whatever riches the scientists discover. The point is to maintain the survival of the human race at all costs, even if it means annihilating indigenous groups such as the Na'vi.

As the chief villain in the movie says, "It isn't over until I am dead," or something to that effect. On this "human" side of Cameron's dialectic, then, there is little sense of a spiritual world beyond the material. Indeed, the very absence of a life beyond the five senses is what drives the human to acquire resources at any cost. This is Darwinism at its most basic level.

Cameron contrasts this hellish vision of humanity with the other side of the dialectic: the Na'vi themselves. These tall, long-limbed, blue-skinned creatures represent the diametric opposite of materialistic humanity. They live in harmony with their world and see the survival of their bodies as subservient to the natural cycles of their ecology. In the network computer language used by the human scientists who understand Pandora, the life energy of the Na'vi are "downloaded" into their bodies at birth, and then "uploaded" back at death into a vast reservoir of collective energy known as Eywa — the Mother Goddess.

If the humans see the body as an end in itself, the Na'vi view it as simply a vehicle for the life energy. As in the classic Hindu understanding, the material world is like a horse on which the soul rides towards eternity.

This dialectic, this opposition between pure materialism and a kind of "spiritism" based on Hindu teaching, present the film's hero, Jake Scully, with a choice. In the human world, he is crippled, unable to walk or afford the operation that would make him whole again. However, as a result of technology invented for the purposes of the movie's plot, his consciousness (his life energy) is downloaded into a body similar to that of the Na'vi — agile, powerful, whole. In that body, he learns and then wholeheartedly embraces their way of life. It is no coincidence that the term "avatar" refers to the Hindu concept of a deity taking on a human form; this is exactly what Jake does when he appears as a Na'vi.

The dilemma that Jake faces, however, is precisely the problem with the film's spiritual vision. In this life, should we really have to choose, as Jake does, between a materialistic, consumerist world in which the body is the be-all and end-all of life, and a "spiritistic" world in which the body is merely a vehicle for the incorporeal spirit or soul?

In the Christian understanding, at least, the answer is no. The human body of Christ was not just another avatar – a human space suit – for the Son of God. Rather, by taking flesh, the Son of God *eternally united* the human body to God's divine identity, and by so doing, He made the human body a sacred space, to be honoured as a temple of the Holy Spirit from conception to burial and beyond, into the resurrection of the body in the age to come.

This teaching is well expressed by the 7th century Father, John of Damascus, who said, "Never will I cease honouring the matter through which my salvation was wrought! I honour it, but not as God… Do not despise matter, for it is not despicable. God has made nothing that is despicable." In other words, we need not choose between obsessing over the material world or rejecting it as a mere vehicle for the spirit. We can respect, honour, cherish and even venerate the body as the very matrix in which God meets us and saves us, while recognizing that the material world is not an end itself, because only the transcendent God can save us.

At the end of *Avatar* (and here comes the spoiler), Jake life energy or spirit or soul or whatever is "uploaded" into a Na'vi body permanently – or at least until his life energy, spirit etc. is "downloaded" again into Eywa when he dies. In effect, he resolves his spiritual dilemma by rejecting the body in which he was born and escaping into another form. In this cop-out lies the fundamental failure of *Avatar*'s spiritual vision, which renders the world far too simplistically and offers "solutions" that constitute little more than an avoidance of the whole gift of life as God has given it – body, soul *and* spirit – with all the struggles, sufferings, handicaps and sacrifices that ultimately make it worth living.

Avatar may be great entertainment, but as far as spiritual nourishment goes, this bag of popcorn won't really satisfy.

January 2010

Mattie J.T. Stepanek and the Vision of Hope

I am currently reading the biography of Mattie J.T. Stepanek, a boy who died of a rare form of muscular dystrophy in 2004. Titled *Messenger*, the book is written by Mattie's mother Jeni, who herself suffers from an adult form of his disease. Before Mattie, she lost three children in infancy and early childhood before doctors finally identified dysautonomic mitochondrial myopathy as a condition she had passed onto them through her genes.

Mattie's life is a chronicle of unbelievable suffering juxtaposed with equally unimaginable beauty, hope and joy. He spent many years of his life in the Paediatric ICU, undergoing countless operations and transfusions. He almost died on several occasions, and spent days in a coma. He lost friends to muscular dystrophy, and when he was three years old, saw his own brother succumb to the disease that would kill him also.

From the beginning, there was no doubt Mattie was going to die. As the years passed, as he continued to survive and even thrive (though confined to a wheelchair and hooked up to a tracheostomy tube and oxygen tank), the urgency to savour each moment became more intense for him and his loved ones, who were all too aware that at any time his trachea (shredded by so many operations) could finally split, drowning him in his own blood.

Mattie's life would be nothing more than a chronicle of loss, pain, suffering and sorrow if it were not for the heroism that he displayed during his short time on earth. At the age of three, he began to compose poems to cope with his brother's death. At twelve, his remarkable character and spirit in the ICU came to the attention of Oprah Winfrey and former President Jimmy Carter. He later travelled the United States, giving talks on his favourite themes: peace and hope. He appeared on *The Oprah Winfrey Show, Larry King Live* and *Good Morning, America*, while his books of poetry rose to the top of *New York Times* bestseller list.

When he died, two weeks before his fourteenth birthday,

hundreds of people attended his funeral. Delivering the eulogy, Jimmy Carter said, "We have known kings and queens, and we've known presidents and prime ministers, but the most extraordinary person whom I have ever known in my life is Mattie Stepanek. His life philosophy was 'Remember to play after every storm!' and his motto was: 'Think Gently, Speak Gently, Live Gently.' He wanted to be remembered as 'a poet, a peacemaker, and a philosopher who played.'"

Though few of us will ever know the kinds of suffering that Mattie and his family experienced, all of us go through periods of loss, pain and sorrow. As I have frequently pointed out, existence itself is a kind of suffering because as human beings, we are naturally subject to forces beyond our control. For people like Mattie, those forces were simply more intense, which made him a true icon by which we can come to terms with our human condition. Specifically, Mattie's story offers us a vision through which we can find hope in the midst of our suffering.

Too often, we think of hope as the possibility that the difficulties and struggles of life might be taken away. We equate hope with escape, and so come to live in expectation of "miracles," by which we mean some unexpected event that will lift our burdens and restore us to "normal" life, whatever we imagine that might look like...

Mattie's life and death show us another way. For him, hope was not about the commutation of an almost-certain death sentence. His vision was more profound and complex, as one of his poems, "Abyss," testifies so eloquently:

> My life is halfway down an abyss,
> A deep, immeasurable space.
> A gulf
> A cavity
> A vast chasm
> My life is not how I planned it to be
> Is not how I want it to be

Is not how I pray for it to be.
In the darkness of this pit
I see a small light of hope.
Is it possible for me
To climb such heights?
To rebuild the bridges?
To find my salvation?
The song in my heart is so quiet
Is so dark
Is so fearful,
I dare not stay in this abyss.
Though deep and vast, I'm only halfway down
Thus I am already halfway up
Let such words fall onto my heart
And raise me from this depth.

I prefer not to analyze these words. What I hear is the poet's heart seeking fulfilment in the midst of an abyss. Hope, for him, is not about escaping the 'vast chasm' as about finding a way to be 'raised up' within it. Hope is his choice to see his suffering as the medium in which to find salvation. I am reminded of another poet, T.S. Eliot, who said, "I have lost my sight, smell, hearing, taste and touch: How should I use them for your closer contact?"

At the beginning of the Orthodox divine liturgy, the priest says, "In the tomb with the body, in Hades with the soul, in paradise with the thief and on the throne of glory were You, O Boundless Christ, filling all things." I am certain Mattie would say 'amen' to these words. His vision of hope is not the longing to escape from our suffering, but the daily choice to ask how we can use our suffering to find ever closer contact with the One who meets us in the midst of death itself. Only then can we truly find divine freedom inside our human bondage, eternal joy inside our temporal sorrow, and heavenly light inside our earthly darkness.

May 2011

Keyholes into Church History

The Story So Far

When I introduce myself as an Orthodox priest, I am often asked the same question: "Orthodox what? Orthodox Jew?" Rather perturbed that the large pectoral cross did not provide any hints, I patiently explain that "Orthodox" means "Eastern Orthodox," and refers to the second largest body of Christians in the world. Orthodox Christianity is the primary understanding of Christians in the Russian Federation, Greece, the Balkan states, the Middle East and (in a slightly wider sense) Ethiopia, Egypt and yes, even India.

But what is Eastern Orthodoxy? What makes it different from Roman Catholicism and various forms of Protestantism? I have no desire in this column to engage in polemics or judgements regarding other Christians. However, I believe it may be useful to begin a little series of articles explaining the origins and development of the Eastern Orthodox Church with a view to filling out the variety of your experiences of Christianity as a whole.

The answer to the question, "What is Eastern Orthodoxy?" is to a large extent a historical matter. So you will pardon me if I indulge in a little story-telling from the past. It's my feeling that a great many who do not know about the Orthodox Church are in such a position because they have heard only part of the story of Christendom.

Here's the part of the story they have heard. Once upon a time, a small band of fisherman went around the Roman Empire telling people that a man named Jesus was the Son of God, that he had lived and taught, been crucified and raised from the dead and had ascended into heaven, and that he would one day return to judge the world. Meanwhile, everyone needed to confess Jesus as lord, be baptised and live a godly life until he returned.

Before they died or were killed by the hostile authorities, the apostles managed to convert a small group of Christians, who met in the catacombs of Rome, where they sang songs and remembered

Jesus' sacrifice with bread and wine (which some say was actually grape juice). Unfortunately, they too suffered at the hands of a hostile pagan establishment, being crucified, thrown to the lions, and horribly tortured for a number of years. Then, for some reason, Emperor Constantine decided to convert to Christianity, legalizing the faith overnight and later making it the official religion of the Roman Empire.

But it was too late for the Empire. Weakened and corrupted by its decadent leaders, it fell to barbarians from the north, who overran western Europe and kicked off the Dark Ages. According to some, Christianity also entered a moral Dark Age at this point. The Church became a mere institution, with a despotic Pope at its head. Corruption flourished, only coming to an end when Martin Luther and the Reformers started Protestantism. Free from the tyranny of the Catholic Church with its dead works, indulgences and idolatries, Christians were once again free to read the Bible in their own languages and to rediscover in its pages a genuine and personal faith in Jesus Christ, much like those early believers.

That's one version anyway. From another point of view, the Roman Catholic Church actually sustained the cultural and religious life of Europe through its Dark Ages, offering a beacon of learning and faith that led to the Renaissance in the 16th century, when Michelangelo, Leonardo and the rest of those geniuses got to work. And in all of this, the Pope was no tyrant, but the direct descendent of the chief Apostle, Peter, to whom Christ gave responsibility for the Church until He returned. Yes, there were good Popes and bad Popes over the years, but the institution itself remained a continuing testimony that the Church has endured and preserved the Faith intact throughout the centuries.

These versions of history are so brief and simplistic as to be almost offensive, but the reality is, it (or something like it, written by Dan Brown) is all that most educated people will ever know of how the Christian faith developed and (in some minds) degenerated. In an age when religious pluralism lies at the centre of so many of our cultural and social conflicts, isn't it time that we educated ourselves a little more thoroughly, at the very least when it comes to the Judeo-Christian background of Canadian history and society?

So I am going to attempt to retell the above story, in a little more detail and from a slightly different point of view, in the hopes of adding a few more dimensions to our collective current experience and knowledge of Christianity.

Along the way, you may learn some rather surprising facts. For instance, were you aware that writings exist documenting Christian practices from as early as 70 A.D., barely one generation after the disciples of Christ? That the Roman Empire did not actually end in the 4th century, but continued and flourished uninterrupted in the East, for over 1100 years? Did you know that Rome was not the centre of the faith, but that there were five ancient centres, each of which added (and continues to add) to the richness of Christian spirituality? And what about the pagan Vladimir, prince of Kiev, who baptized his entire nation in the river Dnieper in 988 A.D., thereby initiating a great flourishing of Christianity for millions of people in Eastern Europe? Concerning those and other tidbits, a lot more next time.

The Eastern Version

In the previous article, I briefly recounted two versions of conventional story of the Christian Church—Protestant and Catholic—that are most familiar to educated people in our society. I promised to retell those stories, adding an Eastern Orthodox dimension to our current collective understanding of Church history. In all of this, my goal is selfish. I hope to save myself from having to answer the inevitable question I am asked when introducing myself as an Orthodox priest: "Orthodox, eh? Orthodox what?"

So here's the beginning of that story. In the early first century A.D., a man named Jesus was crucified under the Roman authorities. Shortly afterwards, his disciples began to claim that they had encountered Jesus risen from the dead, that all should believe in him as the Son of God and be baptised in order to be saved from their sins.

Within three generations, Jesus' followers had preached their message far and wide, establishing communities of "Christians" (literally, "Christ-worshippers") throughout the Mediterranean region of the Roman Empire. These followers, or "Apostles" (literally, "ones who are sent"), had even gone to the extent of writing down their proclamation as Gospels of Jesus' life, death and resurrection. In addition, the letters of certain Apostles were preserved as examples of the apostolic message to specific communities and persons.

Some of these writings would eventually be compiled into the New Testament. For the most part, however, Christians of the first century did not possess the New Testament in any complete form. Their Scriptures were still the Jewish Scriptures—the Law and Prophets—which they interpreted in the light of what Jesus had done and taught (as explained by the Apostles and their appointed teachers).

How did early Christians worship? While we do not know a

lot, we know more than you might think. According to the Acts of the Apostles, "they devoted themselves to the apostles' teaching and fellowship, to the breaking of bread and the prayers." (Acts 2:42) The Apostles taught that Jesus himself had initiated the "breaking of bread," through which Christians partook of his body and blood. (Matt. 26:26-27; Mark 14:22-24; Luke 22:19-20; Luke 24:30) Breaking bread was known as the Eucharist (from the Greek, "I give thanks"), because it took place at the conclusion of the Jewish meal of thanksgiving or blessing in which the main celebrant would give thanks to God for all His works among His people.

Teaching, then, along with the Eucharist, prayers and fellowship, formed the basis of early Christian worship. A late-first-early-second-century Christian document known as the *Didache* (available online at www.ccel.org) adds more detail. For instance, it tells us that Christians fasted on Wednesdays and Fridays (*Didache* 8), that they prayed at regular hours (*Didache* 8:3), that they met every Sunday to celebrate the Eucharist (*Didache* 14) with specific, prescribed prayers for their services (*Didache* 9-10). In addition, they elected as their leaders bishops and deacons (*Didache* 15:1-2) to oversee and serve their communities.

As far as historical sketches go, this is not bad for a time period generally thought to be shrouded in mystery. Still, the exact order of early Christian services are relatively unknown. The New Testament offers almost no details, and we have nothing resembling, say, a service book from the first century. Why is that?

The Apostle Paul points to an answer in his second Epistle to the Thessalonians: "So then, brethren, stand firm and hold to the traditions which you were taught by us, either by word of mouth or by letter." (2 Thess. 2:15) In encouraging his hearers to stand firm in the apostolic proclamations and teachings about Jesus that he delivered to them (see 1 Cor. 11:2), Saint Paul reveals that these traditions could be both written *and* oral. He is transmitting an entire body of apostolic experience that goes beyond what is written.

Our culture so often depends on texts to interact with the world. As a result, it's a real challenge for us to realize that from its inception, Christianity was not constituted by a particular book or collection of texts. Rather, the Christian faith was in a *personal* encounter with the crucified and risen Jesus Christ. And this encounter was handed down to subsequent generations from the Apostles who met him on the road to Emmaus.

This "handing down" or tradition certainly involved the texts of the New Testament and other early writings, but it was more than that. It was also an unwritten practice of prayer, worship and asceticism passed down through demonstration and experience. By participating in this whole way of life, which continues even today, a baptized Christian can personally share in the original apostolic experience of the One who makes himself known in "the breaking of the bread." And that Christian can then go out to proclaim, as the Apostles did so long ago, "The Lord has risen indeed, and has appeared to Simon!"

The Church of the Martyrs

"The blood of Christians is the seed of the Church." It's a shocking and perhaps even offensive statement by one of the early Church fathers. In our day and age, it may conjure up images of fanatics flying planes into buildings or blowing themselves up on crowded subways. The whole idea of martyrdom, shedding one's blood for the sake of religion, stinks of fundamentalist extremism, and most people (especially polite Canadians) would react almost violently to the suggestion that we could or should be martyrs for any cause.

And yet, for almost three hundred years after the Apostles began proclaiming that Christ was "risen indeed," the Christian Church was nothing if not a Church of martyrs. What provoked the persecution of Christians throughout the Roman Empire is too vast a study for this format. A whole host of socio-religious and economic factors are to be blamed. Whatever the causes, the fact remains that until its legalization under the Emperor Constantine, Christianity was an easy scapegoat for wide range of ills in a declining Roman Empire.

For Christians during this period, faith was inseparable from the real possibility of physical martyrdom. More than that, physical torture and death for one's faith was a defining characteristic of Christian identity. How could it be otherwise when the law stated literally that "Christians may not exist" and when simple attendance at a Christian liturgy constituted a capital offense?

While many of today's churches have left behind the legacy of those early days of persecution, Eastern Orthodox tradition still regards the Church as a Church of the martyrs, and martyrdom as a quintessential vocation of all Christians. Not, of course, the grotesque and deformed excuses for "martyrdom" that was 9/11 and other acts of terrorism through the centuries, but rather martyrdom as the Apostles understood and taught it as a result of their encounter with the crucified and risen Jesus Christ.

The word "martyr" comes from the Greek word

"martyrios," meaning "witness." As such, the Apostles saw their first task as that of martyrs — witnesses to the identity of Jesus Christ, the Son of God who was crucified and risen from the dead. "You are witnesses [in the Greek, literally "martyrs"] of these things" (Luke 24:48) and "You shall receive power when the Holy Spirit has come upon you; and you shall be my *witnesses* in Jerusalem and in all Judea and Samaria and to the end of the earth." (Acts 1:8)

This witness certainly did not mean inflicting violence on others. Jesus explicitly forbade his disciples to take up arms, fight and die for his cause. (Matt. 26:52 and John 18:36) An early apologist, writing an open letter to one of the Emperors in the early second century, declares that "[Christians] obey the established laws, but in their own lives they go far beyond what the laws require. They love all men, and by all are persecuted." (*Letter to Diognetus* 5:10-11) Far from being some kind of social, political or military action, Christian martyrdom was to witness to the unfailing love of God, who in Christ was obedient even to death on the cross.

In baptism, Christians participated mystically in the death and resurrection of Christ. They *became* or "put on" Christ spiritually. In doing so, the Christian took on the challenge of dying to selfishness and participating in the self-emptying love of God for the world. And this was martyrdom because it involved dying, not in military conflict, but on the battlefield of personal whims and desires; not for a political or social cause, but for the cause of God's love for the world in Jesus Christ.

For early Christians, however, physical martyrdom set the seal on the spiritual martyrdom to which they were called by virtue of baptism. They refused the political idolatry of burning a pinch of incense to a "divine" Emperor in the same spirit as they would refuse to worship the other idols in their lives: money, sex, and material possessions. And when they were thrown to the lions, crucified, flayed, boiled or chopped into pieces, they submitted to their gruesome deaths in the same spirit as their crucified Lord who said, "Father, forgive them, for they know not what they do" and "into Your hands I commit my spirit." For early Christians, steadfastness to the point of physical death was the ultimate sign of faithfulness to the spiritual life in Christ to which all Christians are called.

It is only appropriate to illustrate with a story of a Christian martyr from the early fourth century, a slave woman named Charitina. Though not yet baptised, she believed in Christ and proclaimed him boldly. When persecutions arose, her master turned her in to the Roman governor, who ordered her hair cut off and burning coals poured over her head. Then she was thrown into a lake to drown. She managed to clamber out, and as she did, cried: "This is my baptism!" In response, the governor ordered her teeth knocked out and her hands and feet cut off. She died shortly afterwards from loss of blood.

It's a shocking story, but no more shocking that recent events we have witnessed, even in our own time. And much like the early centuries of the Christian era, our time too mingles horrendous violence with excesses of laxity, hedonism and amorality. Now more than ever the early experiences of the Church call us to respond as St. Charitina did, neither offering violence in exchange for violence, nor falling prey to moral timidity and passive betrayal of our fundamental beliefs. It's time to find a way between violent conservatism and permissive liberalism. It's time to find the way of the martyrs — the way that will surrender and die to everything for *His* sake, especially *me* and my ego, so that *you* and everyone else can know the love of the One who gave everything for *us*.

Baptizing the Empire

Late in the 3rd century, the Romans divided their immense and unwieldy empire into two portions, the West and the East, each with its own Emperor. A period of political instability and civil war followed soon afterwards, from which the Emperor Constantine emerged triumphant, the sole Emperor of both sides of the Empire.

According to history, Constantine ascribed his victory to the intervention of the Most High God of the Christians, whom he said had appeared to him in a dream before a crucial battle against his rival Maxentius, and exhorted him to inscribe the Greek letters *Chi* and *Rho* (the first two letters of the word "Christ") on his soldiers' shields. Following his victory, Constantine issued the famous Edict of Milan, which forbade the persecution of Christians, and restored their confiscated properties and rights. Constantine himself confessed Christianity, and the age of Christian legitimacy began.

For some, this is the period in which, despite Jesus' promise that "the gates of hell" would not prevail against it (Matt. 16:18), the Church "went to hell in a hand basket." Infected with paganism, legalism and ritualism, the Church "died" for over 1200 years until Martin Luther and the other Reformers resurrected it in the 16th century.

The reality of that period was a little more complicated. Certainly, the Church faced challenges as a result of its "coming of age." With the known world at its feet and unprecedented freedom and power at its disposal, more than one Christian fell prey to worldly corruption.

However, Eastern Orthodox Christians also see this period as a time when the Church faced for the first time a new opportunity to fulfill the Lord's command: "Go therefore and make disciples of all nations, baptizing them in the name of the Father and of the Son and of the Holy Spirit..." (Matt 28:19) Confronted with the baptism of the Roman world, the Church adopted an approach that St. Justin Martyr (ca. 150 A.D.) summed up as follows: "Whatever good has been said of men belongs to us Christians."

In this view, evangelism meant simply reinterpreting the surrounding culture so as to proclaim the Gospel message. If the pagan image of the shepherd carrying a lamb on his shoulders was a symbol of the ideal pastoral life, why could it not also depict Christ the Good Shepherd of his people? If the pagan feast of the birth of invincible sun was celebrated on December 25th, why could not Christians celebrate the birth of Christ on the same day, since He is the all-powerful Light of the Father, the Sun of Righteousness? If the Emperor could be depicted ruling over the world, why could Christians not portray Christ in imperial garb, as the one to whom all authority in heaven or on earth has been given?

The Christian adoption of these and other aspects of pagan Rome was not merely a syncretism — the adoption of pagan beliefs along with their own — but an immense cultural baptism in which art, music, architecture, philosophy and all aspects of society was yoked into proclaiming the Advent of Christ. The theological reasoning was simple: just as Christ had taken on and transfigured fallen human life with the life of God, so too could Christians transform human culture with the life of the Holy Spirit. Human life was not to be rejected as terminally depraved, but rather as something to be healed and filled with the power of God. As St. John of Damascus would say over four hundred years later: "Do not despise matter, for it is not despicable. God has made nothing that is despicable."

In the history of the Eastern Orthodox Church, many examples can be found of evangelism through cultural baptism. Most relevant for us is the approach taken by Russian Orthodox missionaries to North America in the 18th century. Monks and priests came to local nations and rather than rejecting their native spirituality out of hand as demonic or sinful, they sought to establish parallels between native religion and Christian teachings.

The goal was to speak the uniquely Christian message in a language of native spirituality. At the same time, they translated Christian texts into native languages, even going so far as creating the first written alphabets for the Aleut and Tlingit peoples for that purpose!

Contrast this with the missionaries who started the Residential schools in 19th century Canada, with their legacy of cultural genocide, and we can begin to see the present relevance of Church's history following Constantine's conversion. More than anything, this great Christian "coming out" reminds us that the mandate to proclaim the Gospel is not about demonizing "others," whoever they may be; rather, it is about baptizing them: seeing the good in other cultures, then appropriating and using those good things in such a way that they name and proclaim the ultimate Source of their goodness in Christ.

The Standing Challenge

Late in the fourth century, St. Augustine compared the conversion of Constantine and the legalization of Christianity to a fishing expedition in which "both good and bad fishes" were caught in the net of Church. He was referring, of course, to the inevitable decline of general Christian piety as a result of the new worldly freedoms that Christians everywhere were experiencing.

Before Constantine's Edict of Toleration in 314 A.D., confessing the Christian faith was nothing less than social, cultural, religious and literal suicide. You certainly did not "get ahead in life" by becoming a Christian. On the contrary, you pretty much guaranteed that your property and goods would be confiscated, and that you would meet a painful end through a variety of gruesome means.

With the conversion to Christianity of the highest authority in the known world, the situation took an abrupt about-face. Now, conversion to Christianity was fashionable, the thing to do if you wanted to rise in the social and political ranks of the Empire. It was expedient and convenient for everyone to become a Christian.

As a result, not everyone who converted to Christianity did so out of a whole-hearted desire to "take up his Cross" and follow Christ. The martyr's spirit, which had sustained the Church in the early decades and centuries, was now threatened by a strong tendency to laxity and nominalism (paying lip-service to Christianity, rather than demonstrating one's faith through one's life and actions).

Faced with its new challenge to baptize the Empire, how could the Church maintain the fervency of its commitment to Christ? The answer lay with a group of ordinary Christians, who literally walked away from their lives and went to seek Christ in isolation — monastics. By no means the first, the most influential of these radical Christians is undoubtedly Anthony, who along with Pachomius and Athanasius, is widely credited with founding, establishing and promoting monastic Christian culture.

Anthony at first dwelt in the cowshed at the bottom of the garden of his home in Alexandria. As his reputation for piety and prayerfulness grew, however, the constant stream of visitors seeking to inject new fire into their waning faith overwhelmed him, and he retreated into the desert as a hermit. Pachomius later established coenobitic monasticism: like-minded individuals, each following Anthony's example, living in community under the authority of a "Papa" or "Abba" (from which we get the word "Abbot").

Desert monasticism was just what the Church needed, adding a powerful new dimension to a faith that was facing greater and greater temptations to worldliness. It has been referred to as "standing challenge" to the Church in the world, a continual reminder of Jesus' words: "If you would be perfect, go, sell what you possess and give to the poor, and you will have treasure in heaven; and come, follow me." (Matt. 19:21)

The spiritual witness of these early monks has been compiled and is available in books such as *The Lives of the Desert Fathers* and *The Sayings of the Desert Fathers*. These texts are easy to read and powerful in their directness. Just a few examples: "When asked a question, answer. Otherwise, keep silent," says Abba Poemen. Abba Moses says, "Go and sit in your cell and your cell will teach you everything." And Abba Pastor says, "Any trial that comes to us can be conquered by silence."

Today, Christians face many of the same challenges and temptations as they have since they first acquired the State's stamp of approval. Whether or not we believe that the legalization of Christianity utterly corrupted the Church, the fact remains that all Christians must fight to detach themselves from their possessions (materialism); to make their faith something more than "Sunday only" (secularism); to demonstrate their faith in deeds and not just words (nominalism).

For those of us who have chosen to undertake such struggles

in the world, the ancient tradition of desert monasticism challenges us with a radical solution to a worldly threat that seeks to overcome us an any moment. Eastern Orthodox tradition sums up this solution, evolved over centuries of monastic life and practices, in a single word: *Hesychia* — the Way of Inner Stillness.

Through the practice of short, silent prayers like the Jesus Prayer ("Lord Jesus Christ, the Son of God, have mercy upon me, a sinner!"), Hesychia allows Christians living in the world to accomplish inwardly and spiritually what Saints Anthony and Pachomius did outwardly and literally: "walk away" from our slavery to worldly life; go alone into the room of our hearts and close the door; pray to our Father who is in secret (Matt 6:6), so that He who sees in secret can reward us with the one thing needful: His Spirit, His life, His power — and Himself.

Fighting Over Pictures?

Beginning in the 4th century, groups of migrating tribes from Northern Europe moved south, taking over much of what was the western half of the Roman Empire, from Italy to the British Isles, from North Africa to modern day Poland.

With this "Barbarian Invasion," the Roman Empire fell. Europe entered its "Dark Ages," from which it only began to recover in the 9th century under Charlemagne. Until that renaissance of culture and learning, however, civilization would lie in ruins, with memories of its glorious Roman past preserved in lonely Celtic monasteries, like chrysalises in cocoons.

That, at least, is what our history books say, what we're taught even in the first year of university. What many of us don't realize is that the Roman Empire did not actually collapse in the 4th and 5th centuries. While the western half of the Empire did indeed succumb to the northern invaders, the Eastern half of the Empire – encompassing modern Greece, Macedonia, the Balkan states, Turkey, Syria, Armenia, Egypt and Palestine – remained largely intact.

In the early 4th century, the Emperor Constantine moved his capital from Rome to the small town of Byzantium on the Bosphorus. He then proceeded to rename the town after himself – Constantinople – rebuilding it in the image of the old Rome and continuing its Roman way of life in an uninterrupted, if more Christianised, form.

A long line of Eastern Roman (or Byzantine) Emperors followed Constantine. One of the most notable is Justinian, who built the great Church of Holy Wisdom (Haghia Sophia) in Constantinople, and took back many western lands lost to the barbarians. Then came the rise of Islam in the 7th century, which Justinian's successors were unable to withstand. Over the next eight centuries, the Eastern Roman Empire shrank steadily until at last, in 1453, it finally met its end with the Ottoman Turkish conquest of Constantinople.

I mention all these details of history to make the simple point that, while western Europe struggled through its Dark and Middle Ages, the Eastern Roman Empire both lived and thrived as a Christian civilization for over 1100 years. More to the point, this time period also saw the growth and flowering of the spiritual culture of the Eastern Orthodox Church. If we are going to answer the question, what exactly "Orthodox" means, we first need to understand *just how much happened* outside the borders of our western-European-centred historical experience during that millennium.

Take for instance the Iconoclast controversy, about which most western Christians know very little. You may recall from my last article that Christians had embarked on a project of baptizing the surrounding pagan culture, interpreting ancient pantheistic religions in the light of Christ. A part of this endeavour was the baptism of pagan religious imagery, which Christians appropriated to depict their spiritual experience.

During a period in which little or no significant religious art was produced in western Europe, the Eastern Roman Empire witnessed the highly sophisticated production of religious imagery (known as iconography, or "icon-painting" in Greek). The rise of Islam in the 7th century, however, led to controversy. A dynasty of Syrian Emperors, perhaps influenced by Islam's strictures against religious imagery and the tendency of Greek philosophy towards abstractions, prohibited the production and veneration of icons.

The gut spiritual reaction of the general Christian populace throughout the Eastern Roman Empire was violent. Riots rocked the cities. Much theological reflection was undertaken, and in time, treatises were written distinguishing between *latria* (worship), which belonged exclusively to God, and *proskynesis* (veneration) in which a painted religious images act as "windows into heaven," a human means to access the divine.

A leading theologian of the day, John of Damascus, argued

the case for icons as follows: "But now when God is seen in the flesh conversing with men, I make an image of the God whom I see. I do not worship matter; I worship the Creator of matter who became matter for my sake, who willed to take His abode in matter; who worked out my salvation through matter. Never will I cease honouring the matter through which my salvation was wrought!"

After a hundred years of conflict, debate and reflection, the Iconoclast controversy came to an end in the East, with the veneration of icons being upheld as central to the Christian faith in the second council of Nicaea in 787 A.D. Of course, western Europeans knew of nothing of these conflicts, and so ended up rehashing the issue during the Reformation, which took the opposite tack, rejecting the veneration of images as idolatry.

Given our primarily western European experience of history, from which the Iconoclast controversy is missing, it is easy to lose sight of the wider implications and dimensions of the Christian faith. More than merely a fight over pictures, the debate over icons was a serious reflection on what it means to worship God in the flesh. More specifically, it reminds us that our view of "matter" (whether it is the human body or the natural environment) is not limited to a choice between hedonistic idolatry and Puritan denigration; that the created world should be neither worshipped nor rejected, but venerated and honoured as the very medium and instrument in which and through which God came to save us.

For more information on the Eastern Roman Empire and its history, see John Julius Norwich's *A Short History of Byzantium* and Timothy Ware's *The Orthodox Church*.

The Conciliar Spirit

Between the 4th and 15th centuries, while the West underwent in its Dark and Middle Ages, much took place in the Eastern half of the Roman Empire (known also as the Byzantine Empire). Most importantly for this forum, the Church during this time established the principles of its governance, namely, through councils.

The principles of a Church council derive from the New Testament. The Acts of the Apostles, relates how the early Church faced the question as to whether or not gentile Christians should also be circumcised as Jews. After engaging in "no small dissension and debate" (Acts 15:2) with these "Judaizers," the Apostles Paul and Barnabas went up to Jerusalem, where "the apostles and the elders were gathered together to consider this matter." (Acts 15:6) After much debate, the council accepted that baptism alone was sufficient to make the gentiles acceptable before God. A letter was then delivered to the gentile Christians in Antioch, Syria and Cilicia, who received the decision with joy. (Acts 15:31)

Three centuries later, another controversy arose. Arius, a presbyter from Alexandria, began teaching that Jesus was not really the same as God, but rather a quasi-divine being who had been created some time before the beginning of human history. Like the teachings of the Judaizers, Arius' teaching raised no small dissension and debate, which threatened to tear apart the Church even as it emerged into its age of peace.

The new Christian Emperor Constantine, perhaps sensing that political instability would result from this theological division, insisted that the Church leaders meet to resolve their differences in the traditional New Testament manner. So it was that in 325 A.D., a Church council was held in the city of Nicaea. Constantine, though present and involved, did not actively govern the council, leaving that job to the bishops and presbyters under the leadership of a Spanish bishop, Hosias of Cordoba.

The ancient Church historian Eusebius, writing a few years

after the council, recounts the events: "Some began to accuse their neighbours, who defended themselves, and recriminated in their turn. In this manner numberless assertions were put forth by each party, and a violent controversy arose at the very commencement." After much debate, Arius' teaching was condemned and the council reached "one mind and judgment respecting every disputed question." Eusebius adds: "Those points also which were sanctioned by the resolution of the whole body were committed to writing, and received the signature of each several member."

Of course, the issue did not end with the conclusion of the council. The decisions of the bishops and presbyters needed to be presented to Christians throughout the Empire for their approval. This resulted in almost 60 years of further discussion and debate among the general Christian populace, before the decisions of Nicaea were finally accepted as *ecumenical*: universal and binding for all Christians who claimed to follow the faith of the Apostles.

In the centuries that followed, numerous theological divisions resulted in Church councils throughout the Byzantine Empire. Of the many councils held, the Eastern Orthodox Church accepts seven as ecumenical: Nicaea I (325 A.D.), Constantinople I (381 A.D.), Ephesus (431 A.D.), Chalcedon (451 A.D.), Constantinople II and III (553 A.D. and 680 A.D. respectively) and Nicaea II (787 A.D.).

These and other councils followed the general pattern laid down in Acts 15. 1) Dissension arose over particular matters. 2) Church elders and leaders assembled. 3) Debate and discussion ensued. 4) Consensus was finally reached and a decision made. 4) The decision was offered to the faithful for their acceptance. In time, the assembly of the Church either accepted or rejected the councils' decisions, as the Holy Spirit guided them.

In the Eastern Orthodox understanding, Church councils are neither theological commissions that hand down their decisions like laws from on high, nor are they democratic free-for-alls in which a mere 51% majority is accepted as "the will of the people."

They are neither the tyranny of men nor the "rule by numbers."

Rather, councils operate on the assumption that individual Christians (both lay and clerical) have, by virtue of their baptism, received "all the fullness of God" (Eph. 3:19). Through debate and discussion, the people of God strive to articulate the one truth of God that lies within them. And as they move towards this consensus, like spokes moving towards the centre of a wheel, they are united in "one Lord, one faith, one baptism, one God and Father of us all, who is above all and through all and in all." (Eph. 4:5-6)

Church history clearly demonstrates that finding such God-inspired consensus (known as *conciliarity*) is always a messy and protracted process. But it is *necessarily* so. For only when God's people take the time required to internalize and articulate the one truth in diverse and unique voices, can they fully reveal the life of the Trinity itself, where one God is made known in three Persons: unity in diversity, and diversity in unity.

The Gospel to the Slavs

Beginning in the 8th century, the Slavic tribes of what is now modern Belarus, Russia and Ukraine invited a handful of Viking warriors to rule over them. These Vikings (also known as Varangians) established a medieval state known as the Kievan Rus.

After two centuries of forceful and bloody rule, one Rusyn warrior named Vladimir emerged as supreme, and established himself as the grand prince of Kiev. Having consolidated his power over the Slavs, Vladimir made a historic decision: he decided to get a religion for his people. Of course, the Slavs had a pantheistic set of beliefs, but Vladimir felt that this homemade religion would do little to gain recognition for his people among the other great empires of the earth. What he needed was a recognized faith.

A 12th century document known as the "Primary Chronicle" or *The Chronicle of Nestor*, records Vladimir's search for a national religion. He sent emissaries to explore the religions of neighbouring nations: to the German Christians in western Europe, to the Muslim Bulgarians, and to the Eastern Orthodox Byzantines of Constantinople. He even received a delegations of Jewish Khazars, in order to enquire about Judaism.

According to the *Chronicle*, Vladimir rejected western Christianity because it was "too gloomy"; Islam because of its restrictions against alcohol, which Vladimir characterized as "the joy of the Rus"; and Judaism because he saw the loss of Jerusalem as a sign of their being "abandoned by God." When his emissaries returned from Constantinople, however, they excitedly described the worship of the Byzantine Church: "We no longer knew whether we were in heaven or on earth, nor such beauty, and we know not how to tell of it."

Whether he was motivated by the beauty of Byzantine worship, or by some other more political motive, Vladimir chose Byzantine Christianity for both himself and his people. He received baptism, and married a Byzantine princess. He tore down the pagan temples of his people, and built churches in their place. He ordered a statue of the supreme Slavic god Perun to be thrown into the Dnieper river. Finally, he ordered the residents of Kiev to come down to the Dnieper, where they were to receive baptism as he had done.

The *Chronicle* records this iconic event in the following way: "Vladimir made known throughout his village: 'Those who day after tomorrow do not appear on the bank of the river, rich or poor, will be considered as rebels and traitors.' The day following Vladimir accompanied by the priests, those of the empress and those of Kherson, went to the Dnieper, where there was gathered an innumerable crowd of men who entered into the water, some up to the neck, others only to the chest. The children stayed on the bank and were covered with water; some plunged into the river. Others swam here and there while the priests read their prayers. And this formed a spectacle tremendously curious and beautiful to see. At last, when all the people were baptized, each returned to his home."

Left to Vladimir's heavy-handed methods (he was a Viking, after all), the Slavs may never have taken to Christianity. However, the Byzantine missionaries who came to catechize the newly Christianized people did so not by force, but through cultural baptism, a process I have spoken about in a previous article. Here again, six centuries after Christianity first appropriated pagan Roman culture for its own purposes, was a sensibility that insisted on the inherent value of local culture and spiritual traditions, and attempted to translate Christianity into those contexts, rather than imposing it at the point of the sword.

Most significant among these efforts was the creation of a written form of the Slavic language of Vladimir's people. The Cyrillic alphabet, so named after one of its originators, Cyril, a Byzantine missionary monk, was used to transcribe Old Slavonic, and render the Scriptures in a language the people could understand.

So effective were these methods that eight centuries later, a group of Russian missionaries sent to North America brought with them an inherent respect for native cultures. Arriving in Alaska, the Russian missionary monks simply re-enacted the process that their ancestors had experienced: they sought to live with and understand the First Nations they found: the Yupik, the Aleut, and the Tlingit nations of the Northwest. Indeed, such Russian missionaries as Innocent Veniaminov even imitated Cyril, and created a written form of Tlingit in which he could write the Gospels for teaching purposes.

Contrast this with Protestant missionaries who appeared one century later, destroying native language and culture, and we can see the historical significance of the mass conversion of Slavs in the 10th century. We can see that winning people to belief is not accomplished by political force driven by a vision of nation or Empire. Rather, it is a matter of speaking to minds and hearts in a language that can be understood. This conversation begins with literal spoken language, of course, but it goes beyond that. It also means speaking the language of a people's way of life, which can only be learned by living among them. And ultimately, it means speaking the universal language of love, the language of the One who spoke the language of human existence so that we might speak the language of God.

For more information on Eastern Orthodoxy in Alaska, see Michael Oleksa's excellent book *Orthodox Alaska*.

The Great Schism

When I introduce myself as an Orthodox Christian, the most common response is "Orthodox what?" The second most common response is "Orthodox? That's like Catholic, right?"

What's the difference between Eastern Orthodoxy and Roman Catholicism? Like so many other questions I have explored in this series, the answer is a matter of history. In 1054 A.D., a papal delegate, Cardinal Humbert, arrived in Constantinople from Rome to excommunicate the Patriarch of Constantinople and the entire Eastern Orthodox Church. Known as "the Great Schism," this date marks the official split between the two churches, which has not yet been healed.

How did it comes to this? Flash back six hundred years or more, to a period when no real distinction could be made between "Roman Catholic" and "Orthodox." There was only the Church made of dioceses in urban centres throughout the Empire, each headed by a bishop who governed, along with his presbyters and deacons.

Bishops who ruled the largest cities (like Alexandria and Constantinople), or centres of spiritual distinction (like Rome, Jerusalem and Antioch), took on a special prominence. Among these, Rome was preeminent. Both Saints Peter and Paul had been martyred there, and Saint Peter was Rome's first bishop. In addition, Roman Christians had a reputation for solid theology. The opinion of the bishop of Rome (also known as the Pope, which means literally "Papa") was highly regarded, and in matters of dispute, Rome regularly offered wise and godly arbitration.

Despite his moral authority, however, the Pope did not interfere (at least in the early days) in the jurisdictions of other bishops. They often sought his opinion, but they did not need his approval to make decisions within their own dioceses. In fact, all bishops were equal by virtue of their consecration, whether they ruled prestigious urban centres or small cow towns. The governance of the Church was not the prerogative of a single individual, but of all the bishops, who acted in council with the approval of the laity.

Then Germanic tribes invaded from the north, cutting off western Europe (which happened to be the diocese of the bishop of Rome) from the rest of the Empire, including all the remaining dioceses (Alexandria, Constantinople, Jerusalem and Antioch among them). Communication between East and West virtually ceased.

Now in isolation, the western half of the Church faced unique problems. When Germanic converts to Christianity fell into Arianism (a heresy that denied the full equal divinity of Jesus with God the Father), Spanish theologians proposed an addition to the 4th century Nicene Creed. Where the original version said that the Holy Spirit "proceeded from the Father," the revised version stated that the Holy Spirit "proceeded from the Father *and the Son.*" By adding this clause (known as *filioque*), the theologians hoped to equate the authority of Jesus with God the Father, and refute the Arians.

Another unique western controversy centred around investiture. According to custom, a newly-consecrated bishop would received his staff and ring from the local lord on whose land the diocese was located. This "lay investiture" was in effect the state's approval of Church authority. However, because Germanic legal traditions gave the lord possession over anything on his land, the lords felt that they could invest only those bishops they preferred, like their relatives or political favourites...

In reaction to these nepotistic abuses, the Pope asserted his supreme jurisdictional authority over the Church, including all Church appointments, quite separate from state approval. Anyone who disagreed would be excommunicated.

Remember, these controversies and their solutions took place in the *West*, completely isolated from the East, which faced its own difficulties and conflicts (such as the Iconoclasm, as discussed in a previous article). In fact, neither side of the Empire had any real sense of what was happening in the other, and only when western Europe emerged from its Dark Ages into some semblance of social and political stability, did westerners encounter — or rather, collide with — the East, with tragic consequences.

Having been cut off from the East, western theologians assumed that their western problems and solutions applied to everyone. The *filioque* was not just a local response to a local heresy; everyone needed to accept it. The jurisdictional authority of the Pope was not just absolute in the diocese of the West; it was absolute *everywhere*, in the whole of Christendom, on pain of excommunication!

For their part, the Eastern Orthodox theologians were stuck in their Byzantine Greek style of theology. They dismissed their western brethren as barbaric and irrelevant. With both sides refusing to understand one another, we arrive at that fated day in 1054, when Cardinal Humbert flung down the papal bull of excommunication on the altar of Haghia Sophia, and stormed out in a self-righteous huff. The Patriarch of Constantinople's excommunication of the Pope followed as a matter of course.

The division between the East and the West was not by any means sealed in 1054 A.D. Only in the 13th century, when Roman Catholic knights of the Fourth Crusade sacked and burned Constantinople, killing and raping its Eastern Orthodox citizens, was the separation between the two churches finally cemented with Christian blood.

Today, both Roman Catholic and Eastern Orthodox theologians are striving to heal the wounds inflicted ten centuries ago. Their task is an immense one. Not only have the two churches have evolved different theological, liturgical, and spiritual traditions, they have embedded themselves into distinct cultural attitudes. The two churches share much, but often have very different understandings of what they share.

If reunion is to come, though, it will not come from

theologians working in ivory towers. My brief history shows that real unity will come from ordinary people striving to understand what happened to cause their divisions; learning each other's cultural languages; respecting legitimate differences of experience, while striving for common ground in the Lord who prayed that "they may be one, even as we are one." (John 17:11)

A Personal History

Until now, I have attempted to provide a view of Church history that expands on the Reader's Digest versions that we too often receive. The final result has been less a panorama than a few select keyholes into the past, which I hope will open new doors of understanding of Christianity and specifically, of Eastern Orthodoxy. At the very least, I hope that I can introduce myself as an Orthodox priest with fewer incidences of the inevitable reaction: "Orthodox what?"

So much more could be said. This series, in fact, could extend for many more years come. Early church history can and does consume entire books. The 1100 years of Byzantine history fills bookshelves. The history of Russia and the other Slavic nations occupy armies of scholars. And I have barely touched the vast array of topics in Eastern Orthodox theology and spirituality, from iconography to monasticism, from the Jesus prayer to the Divine Liturgy...

I have decided to leave the details of the above topics to those who can do them a little more justice. For instance, an overview of Orthodox Church history and teaching can be found in Timothy Ware's book *The Orthodox Church*, which is both authoritative and accessible to the non-scholarly reader.

I would like to end this series on a personal note: how did I end up as an Eastern Orthodox Christian? What was it about this rather strange faith that originally attracted me and that now commands my devotion and service?

A personal history of my religious background is in order. I was born in the Seychelles, to a Roman Catholic mother and an Anglican father. At the insistence of my mother's parents, I was christened Roman Catholic.

In 1979, we left the Seychelles and spent the next 10 years living in East and Southern Africa. During this period my religious experiences were more Protestant than Catholic. My father would bring my sister and I to Sunday school at whatever denomination was convenient, and pick us up afterwards.

1989 saw us immigrate to Canada. Then in my early teens, I was tending towards spiritual rebelliousness. My father, however, insisted that I be confirmed Anglican, in the tradition of his family. Then, he said, I could do what I wanted. I acquiesced with bad grace. After Confirmation, I dropped out of Christianity and sought the dubious pleasures of a purely secular, hedonistic lifestyle.

By God's providence, however, I proved to be a very bad hedonist, which I now credit to persistent Catholic guilt. Having failed to live a dissolute life, I found myself in an emotional and spiritual crisis. At the time, I was working for a couple who were Evangelical Protestants. They had been trying to get me to become a Christian for a while, but it was not until I "hit bottom" that I finally paid attention to their message: "God loves you. Otherwise He would not have sent His Son to die for you."

I dedicated my life to Christ from then on. I roamed in Evangelical circles for a while, but was uncomfortable with the hyper-emotionalism. Finally, I rediscovered my roots and joined the Anglican community of St. John's in Shaughnessy, Vancouver.

It was then I encountered the Orthodox Church. One night in 1993, I was at a poetry reading in Vancouver, and met a young man, who (like me) was an aspiring poet taking a B.A. in English Literature at UBC. He invited me and my friends to his church: Saint Herman of Alaska Orthodox Church.

My first experiences of Orthodoxy were strange. This church had no pews, only benches lining the walls. There were no drums, bass, guitars, or even a piano; worship was chanted in harmony. Every service was lit by candles and fragrant with incense. And most troubling of all, communion was restricted to those who accepted the teachings of the Orthodox Church.

I struggled for months with this Orthodox "all or nothing" mentality. I was interested in the worship, which claimed to derive from the first century, but I was not sure I wanted to make the commitment required to participate.

I might have waffled a good deal longer had not Michael Ingham, the Anglican bishop of New Westminster, come to my Anglican Church on Easter of 1993, and denied the resurrection. That's when I knew I had to find a spiritual home whose essential doctrine and practice had remained consistent from the beginning. Unable to accept the Catholic doctrine of papal infallibility, I had to decide whether the intense, strange Orthodox Church was some weird cult, or the real spiritual home for which I was longing.

I must confess that given the significance of the decision, I was rather impulsive. I read only one book about Orthodoxy (and not a very good one at that). I listened to the witness of my best friend (who became Orthodox before I did) and the loving attitude of St. Herman's community. I attended more services, got used to the strangeness, and fell in love with the dignity and beauty of Orthodox worship. I asked questions, thought through the answers, and found them acceptable. I made the commitment.

In fact, I took the right approach, for the Eastern Orthodox Church is best understood through a direct experience with its worship and fellowship. Newspaper articles are useful as far as they go, but Christianity is less about knowing a text (central as the Bible text is) than a person: the person of Jesus Christ crucified and raised from the dead. Encountering Eastern Orthodoxy is likewise a personal matter, which means simply meeting and praying with Orthodox Christians with an eye to growing in one's understanding of the community. As I conclude this reflection of aspects of Church history, therefore, I would invite you to come and see what Eastern Orthodoxy is all about and discover a whole new dimension to a faith that has endured since the beginning.

The Sanctification of Time

A Date with Eternity

We sometimes hear that December 25th is not originally a Christian holiday. According to this argument, the Emperor Aurelian instituted a pagan holiday celebrating the birth of *Sol Invictus*, "the Invincible Sun," in A.D. 274.

In this view, the Christians appropriated this date in an effort to uproot and supplant pagan beliefs with their own. The December 25th date, we are told, is actually nothing more than Christian propaganda, one more example of just how oppressive the Church can be to groups who disagree with them.

A bit more investigation, though, shows this argument to be only skin deep. Most scholars now agree that Christians chose December 25th as Christ's birthday long before Emperor Aurelian instituted his pagan feast.

According to an ancient Jewish belief (which Christians inherited), a prophet died on the same day as he was conceived. Early Christians, who held that Christ was crucified on March 25th, therefore assumed he was conceived on the same day, when the angel Gabriel announced his birth to the Virgin Mary.

Indeed, both Roman Catholic and Eastern Orthodox churches still celebrate the Annunciation—Jesus' conception by the Holy Spirit—on March 25th. By ancient logic, then, Jesus would have been born nine months after March 25th, on—you guessed it—December 25th.

But the quarrel over actual dates misses a bigger point. By associating Jesus' conception and birth with his death, the ancient Christians affirmed something crucial about the good news of Christianity. We find this fundamental truth articulated in one of the Orthodox Christmas hymns:

> *Today the Virgin comes to the cave*
> *Where she will give birth to the Eternal Word.*
> *Hear the glad tidings and rejoice, O universe!*
> *With the angels and shepherds glorify Him who reveals Himself:*

The eternal God, a little child!

The Nativity of Christ is the beginning of God's great work among His people, a work completed with His death on the Cross and resurrection on the third day. Taken together, the conception, birth, life, death and resurrection of Christ constitute the very heart of the joyous Christian proclamation: that in Jesus Christ, the eternal God—transcendent, unapproachable and all-powerful—has come to unite Himself to us and so unite us to Himself, freeing us from death and sin, and making us "partakers of divine nature," (2 Peter 1:4) As St. Athanasius the Great declared most boldly: "God became man, so that man could become God."

December 25th, then, is not just another example of Christian oppression. It is not just a date to remember a past event. Rather, December 25th is another opportunity bring into the present time the eternal reality of Immanuel: "God with us" from birth to death and resurrection. This Christmas, then, we can all rejoice in that joy once again, celebrating the moment when God Himself broke into history, in the final act of His mysterious, incomprehensible, infinite love for us.

December 2009

A Second Run at Easter

It happens every year around Christmas or Easter: *Time* or *Newsweek* publishes yet another article on Jesus claiming to offer 'new' evidence that contradicts the claims of traditional Christianity. The same old line-up of scholars marches in to repeat the same old mantra: whoever the 'real' Jesus was, He did almost nothing ascribed to Him in the Gospels, including rise from the dead. All of that divine stuff was foisted on the world by His deceptive disciples who refashioned a simple rabbi from Nazareth into the spokesman for the greatest purveyor of institutional oppression since the KGB.

This year has been no different. In the March 31st issue of *Maclean's,* entitled, "Jesus Has An Identity Crisis," reader's are offered not only the same old promise of "new doubt" cast on the divinity of Jesus, but the additional suggestion that "the Church would be better off without Him." The article's most priceless moment, though, comes when it quotes United Church minister Gretta Vosper as saying, "Why do we need a 'revolutionary' voice from two millennia ago? We have fabulous ideas of our own."

Why indeed? Why, given all this 'new doubt,' do faithful Christians continue to believe in their crucified and risen Lord, and why is traditional Christian faith continuing to grow in large parts of the world? Is it really because most Christians have switched off their brains and closed their eyes? Perhaps I am just speaking as a mindless minion of the Church here, but there's a little more to it than that.

For many theologians, faith in Christ (or lack of it) is primarily an archaeological event, like digging for dinosaur bones. Somewhere in the Gospels is buried the "historical Jesus," by which is meant "Jesus as he really was." Using various sophisticated techniques, the scholars clear away what they believe is superfluous material to discover the "original" teachings and acts of Jesus. Once unearthed, He may well be uninspiring or irrelevant, at which point the scholars can decide whether or not to dispose of Him…

For most believing Christians, however, faith is not archaeological event as much as a living encounter with the person of Christ. A cursory examination of the four Gospels reveals that they are essentially personal testimonials to the true identity of Jesus. The texts certainly contain history, but only as the medium through which the writers could accomplish a more important task: bearing witness to their encounters with Jesus after His resurrection, when they finally understood that He is the Son of God (see Luke 24:13-35).

What those post-resurrection encounters might have looked like if you had tried to capture them on video is a matter of speculation. The fact remains, however, that *something* happened after the crucifixion to turn a group of fearful, ignorant Palestinian peasants into a force that even Imperial Rome could not withstand. The Gospels were the fruit of this transformation, and whatever one might say about their presentation of Jesus, it was clearly infectious. The generation that followed the apostles sacrificed wealth, power, prestige and even their own lives on the basis of their Gospel testimonies. And those faithful ones in turn inspired others to similar acts, handing down their convictions through the centuries to the present day, when ordinary people of faith still embody the original apostolic encounter by proclaiming "Christ is risen!" and making daily life choices on the basis of that proclamation.

The identity of Jesus, then, does not depend on murky archaeological evidence or abstruse scholarly methods, but on a living chain of witnesses, beginning with the apostles and extending down to the present moment. Jesus is not an artifact to be freed from later accretions, like some dusty fossil. He is really present in the transfigured lives of those who put their trust in him. When I see a person overcome a crushing addiction or heal a broken marriage by putting their faith in the risen Christ, I know that the chain of apostolic experience is intact. And this in turn reaffirms my conviction that the original encounter between the risen Christ and His apostles *was* truly genuine. A life transformed in His name today is the most convincing proof of what they proclaimed about Him two thousand years ago.

This year, one third of the world's Christians (known as the Eastern Orthodox Church) will celebrate Easter or *Pascha* following a tradition that places the Passion of Christ after the Jewish Passover. As we approach this "Second Easter," I invite you also to take a second look at the *meaning* of Easter: not as a time for wallowing in 'new doubt' and despair, but as an new opportunity to encounter the Jesus Christ who rose then and who is risen now — really, truly, physically risen *now* in the hope and joy-filled lives of all his faithful ones.

April 2008

The Ancestors of God

You may have, at some time in your life, looked into the genealogy of your family. There are a number of reasons why we do things like this. One of them may be that at some level we hope to be related to royalty...

Which means, of course, that we are disappointed most of the time. Inevitably, we discover that our ancestors came from very ordinary stock, and if we are related to royalty, it is usually in a disreputable way, such as our great-great-great-great-grandmother being the illegitimate daughter of a duke or something...

The quest for a genealogy is motivated by a desire for identity. Who am I? Where do I come from? More profoundly still, where do I belong? What is my worth? Genealogical quests aside, we all ask ourselves these questions, and we often try to answer them out of our own heads, constructing ideals for ourselves based on work, school, family, and even religion. We live our lives in a constant state of trying to fulfill these ideals, and like the results of a genealogical search, we are often disappointed in our own limitations.

On the Sunday prior to Christmas, the Orthodox Church lectionary prescribes Matthew 1:1-25: the genealogy of Jesus Christ, also known as "the ancestors of God." On first glance, this genealogy is a royal genealogy much like the one we may have hoped for ourselves. We hear distinguished names like Abraham, Isaac, Jacob, Judah, David, and Solomon, and Jesus appears at the end of this noble list as a king in a long line of kings, an exalted personage in a long line of exalted personages.

And yet on closer reading, something is strange about this particular genealogy. It mentions women, which most traditional genealogies in the Ancient Near East would not have done. There is Tamar, who allowed Judah to use her as a harlot in order that he might realize that he had done her wrong when he did not give her in marriage to his son Shelah, but instead kept her as a widow without children in his house. (Genesis 38) There is Rahab, whose name echoes that of the harlot who lived in the walls of Jericho and who was counted among the righteous because she gave a friendly welcome to Israelite spies. (Joshua 2) There is Ruth, the Moabitess, who left her homeland and seduced Boaz in order to gain his protection as the next of kin. There is Bathsheba, the wife of Uriah the Hittite, who was taken into adultery by David. Finally, we are told of Mary, who is found with child and therefore is assumed to have committed adultery, but who gains the protection of Joseph, who bestows his Davidic lineage on his son Jesus.

On a first, literal level, then, the genealogy reveals that, despite the unusual circumstances of his birth, Jesus is the promised Messiah, in the line of David by adoption. On a more profound level, however, the genealogy tells us that the kingship of Christ originates in spiritual outsiders—those who were called harlots but who proved to be righteous because of their steadfast faith in God and His Word. And Jesus is the culmination of this lineage of faith in the face of marginalization. Jesus too was rejected from the world, crucificied as a condemned and excluded criminal, but because of His obedience even to death on the cross, God exalted Him as a king before whom all should bow. (Phil. 2:5-10)

What does this mean for us? Simply that we need no longer rest our self-worth on our worldly reputation. We need no longer ask ourselves, how am I appearing to so-and-so? How should I really be and how close am I to that ideal? Rather, we need only embrace our human weakness and frailty, rejecting the ideals of confidence and strength that our world so loves to promote. For the "ancestors of God," who produced God in the flesh Himself, witness that even if the world excludes and rejects us, God will raise us up and grant us the royal lineage we have always desired, making us co-heirs and co-rulers in the Kingdom of Heaven.

December 2008

Annunciation

In both Eastern and Western liturgical traditions, March 25th marks a special event in the life of Jesus Christ: His conception in the womb of the Virgin Mary. This event is also known as the Annunciation, when according to the Gospel of St. Luke, the Archangel Gabriel came to the Virgin and announced, "Do not be afraid, Mary, for you have found favor with God. And behold, you will conceive in your womb and bear a son, and you shall call his name Jesus." (Luke 1:30-31)

Mary's response to this announcement is a familiar and beloved one: "Behold, I am the handmaid of the Lord; let it be to me according to your word." (Luke 1:38) According to Church tradition, her words of acceptance were what allowed God's Word to enter and initiate within her the human conception of her Son.

Less well known is *why* March 25th is the date of the Annunciation. Some scholars argue that Christian chose the pagan feast of *Sol Invictus* ("the Invincible Sun") on December 25th to celebrate the birth of Jesus. As a result, the feast of Jesus' conception was established nine months earlier on—you guessed it—March 25th.

This line of argumentation has recently been replaced by a more interesting explanation. Scholars now suggest that some early Christians believed that Jesus actually died on March 25th. And because they ascribed to Him the ancient Jewish piety that a prophet died on the same day as he was conceived, they also established the date for His conception. While the celebration of Jesus' death later shifted, becoming dependent on the lunar cycle, the Annunciation remained fixed, with Christmas nine months later.

Whether this explanation is ultimately factual, I neither know nor care; entertaining its possibility does, however, offer a rich opportunity for reflection. If Jesus did die on the same day as He was conceived, then from the moment of His conception, He was *destined* to die. Further, if Jesus is the pattern after which every human being is supposed to be made, then you and I are also born to die, as He was.

This is more than just to say that one day, all of us are going to die. The coincidence of Jesus' conception and His death suggest to that the *purpose* of our existence is to die, not just "in the end," but every day, moment by moment. Just as Jesus' ultimate death coincided with His conception, every instant of my life must also coincide with a death—an offering of myself for others without concern for my own welfare.

Frankly, the world around us takes the opposite tack. We are born, are taught to survive, are filled with knowledge and skills, find jobs and careers, acquire wealth and material possessions, invest, save money for day—all so that we can manage our destinies, if not completely then a little *more* completely than before.

Beneath that imperative to manage and control is a more primeval impulse: the fear of death, over which we have no control. The need to survive, to cheat death or put it off for as long as possible is the ultimate driving force behind almost every aspect of individual, social, economic and political life in this world.

The Annunciation, linked with the Cross, is a flat out rejection of this Darwinian way of thinking. When I affirm that my life is a series of deaths to self, I choose something other than "survival of the fittest" and "kill or be killed." Rather, I make choices as a consumer, as a parent, as a spouse, as a citizen, as a member of the Church, that benefit someone other than myself. I am willing to take cuts, live with less, deprive myself of comforts and conveniences, so that other individuals, communities, species, the world outside myself—might survive and thrive. It's counterintuitive and revolutionary.

Am I destroyed when I make the decision to make my life choices a series of little deaths? By no means. After all, if I die to myself so that you might live, and you die to yourself so that I might live, we both end up, not just alive, but enriched by one another's lives. And even if you refuse to respond in kind to my act of self-sacrifice, I can still choose to die in imitation of Jesus' own self-emptying death for me and the entire human race, and in doing so, I find myself resurrected and transformed by a *His* resurrection.

The Annunciation, then, is a call to death, but not destruction. It is a challenge to relinquish fear, to reject self-interest, to demonstrate the courage and the conviction of the Virgin Mary's simple acceptance of Gabriel's announcement, trusting like her that though the water may come up over our heads, God will not allow us to be drowned in our sufferings, but will lead us through into the promised land of life and joy.

March 2010

The Blessing of Waters

In the liturgical calendar of the Eastern Orthodox Church, January 6th marks the feast of Theophany (also known as Epiphany in the West), which commemorates the baptism of Jesus Christ in the river Jordan by the prophet John (known also as the Forerunner, because he prophesied the coming of Christ). Theophany marks the end of the Christmas season, which you may know as the 12 days of Christmas, the period of time in which the good news of "God with us" is revealed to the world.

Not surprisingly, the central image of Theophany is that of water. In the Scriptures, water is a powerful symbol, being referred to over 600 times in a wide variety of contexts. The feast of Theophany, in which God Himself enters into the waters of the Jordan, is the culmination of the meaning of water throughout the Bible.

For the people of the ancient Near East, water had a dual significance. Primarily, it was a primordial and destructive element. God created the world as a kind of "bubble" of order and life in the midst of the waters. The sky was a solid dome above which were "the waters above the heavens." (Genesis 1:6-7) The earth rested upon the waters, on pillars sunk into the deep. (see Psalm 136:6 and 1 Samuel 2:8) And waters encircled the world, raging at its boundaries. (Job 38:8-11)

According to the Scriptures, God's hand held back the waters, which allowed His good creation to continue existing in peace and order. However, when God wanted to chastise His people, to remind them of what things would be like without Him, He allowed the waters to cover the world again. The most prominent example, of course, is the Great Flood that only Noah, his family and his ark of living creatures survived.

In addition, we hear Jonah using water as a metaphor for God's punishment of his disobedience: "For You cast me into the

144

deep, into the heart of the seas, and the flood was round about me; all Your waves and Your billows passed over me." (Jonah 2:3) And the Psalmist echoes a similar sentiment: "Save me, O God! For the waters have come up to my neck. I sink in deep mire, where there is no foothold; I have come into deep waters, and the flood sweeps over me." (Psalm 69:1-2)

Water, then, is the scriptural image of what happens where God withdraws His hand from us. In a broader sense, it represents all of our human sufferings, those parts of our life that are uncertain, messy, difficult, frustrating; those circumstances that do not go as expected or wanted, that lie beyond our control, that defy our attempts to make them submit, to come to order or conform to our expectations. The waters symbolize those events that disturb us, upset us, or shake us up.

But if, in the Scriptures, the waters embody primeval chaos, destruction and death—humanity without God's providential care —then they are also the source of life for the world. In the creation account, the waters brought forth "swarms of living creatures." (Genesis 1:20) As the divine Gardener, God uses the waters to bring life to plants and animals. (Psalm 104: 12-16) Water gushing from the rock at Meribah sustained the people of Israel in the wilderness. (Exodus 17:7) In the Scriptures, water is death and water is life, both at the same time.

This dual significance of water in the Scriptures is fulfilled in the incarnation and baptism of Christ. On one hand, Christ descends into the waters of a world separated from God, submitting Himself to suffering and death out of love for humanity. On the other hand, the waters become the wellspring of eternal life when Jesus emerges and is revealed as the beloved Son of God (Matt. 3:17) who would rise from the dead and deliver creation from the forces of eternal destruction.

In the end, the theological point of Theophany is simple: the sufferings and sorrows of human life are the very wellsprings where God appears to us and embraces us. Far from being a distant deity, cold and unfeeling, God comes to share and transform and redeem the messes and pains of our world from the inside out.

In honour of this season, Orthodox churches throughout the world bless water in all its forms, from lakes and rivers, to streams and ponds. The Church also sprinkles the blessed waters in homes, offices and other places where human beings go about the daily business of life. This year, I am available to bless your home. You don't have to be an Orthodox Christian, or even a Christian of any sort. You need only be willing to believe that somehow, God loves us enough to enter the bitter waters of our human life, and transform it by His coming into the sweetness of divinity.

January 2009

Happy New Year!

Like the beginning of the school year, September marks the beginning of the ecclesiastical (Church) new year. Unlike the secular world, the Church has always followed the pattern of agrarian life, from end of harvest to end of harvest. With all of summer's bounty collected and stored, the people of antiquity, replenished and replete, would prepare themselves for the beginning of a new growing cycle.

As modern folks, we have mostly lost touch with this natural pattern of time. Faint echoes of it remain to us if we grow gardens, but when it comes right down to it, our survival does not ultimately rest on the rhythm of planting, harvesting, and storing. After all, even if our garden fails to produce, there is always the local grocery store...

And yet some of that ancient rhythm is still very much present in our lives, at least psychologically. We may not harvest literal crops in summer, but we do go on vacations or take things a little easier, growing, gathering and storing our personal resources, so that (ideally), we can arrive at September with our mental and spiritual storehouses refilled to brimming, ready to face the coming months.

September is often a time of decisions. How will we use the resources we have regained and stored up during the summer? What activities will we embark on for the fall, winter and spring? For many, this is a time to sign the kids for soccer or piano lessons, or consider involvement in church or other community activities.

And of course, the temptation every year is to fill our calendar to overflowing. Having received another year of life, we want to use it to its fullest potential, which usually means making ourselves incredibly busy with this or that commitment. We not only "seize the day"; we cram with activity until it has no room left to breathe.

The Eastern Church calendar offers an alternate vision to the frenetic pace we so often impose on our year. In the reading prescribed for this coming Sunday, for instance, a wealthy synagogue ruler comes to Jesus and asks, "Good Teacher, what shall I do to inherit eternal life?" Jesus' response? "One thing you still lack. Sell all that you have and distribute to the poor, and you will have treasure in heaven; and come, follow me." (Luke 18)

Like the rest of us approaching a new year with our stock of resources overflowing, the ruler wonders how can he invest and multiply his resources in a way that will benefit him the most. Jesus tells him to make do with less. He challenges him to use all his resources to show forth God's love for the poor ones of the earth, and to foster a greater awareness of and dependence on the One who crowns the year with His bounty and sustains all things with His mighty hand. (see Psalm 65:11)

So perhaps the boldest and most significant decision we can make for the coming year is the decision to do a little *less*. Other than the absolute necessities, make one or two commitments to benefit people other than ourselves. Then leave lots of time for quiet and silence; for meditation and prayer; for walks after a fresh snowfall; for evenings with a nourishing book far from the "idiot box." Time to savor everything we have been given, and praise the One who gave it. We come to September with an abundant harvest of time and energy. Let's make the bounty count for something.

September 2008

The Pentecostal Spirit

Fifty days following Easter, the Orthodox Church celebrates the feast of Pentecost (Pentecost means simply 'the fiftieth day').

The events of Pentecost are described in the Acts of the Apostles. Fulfilling Christ's promise before His death and after His resurrection, the Holy Spirit descended upon the Apostles in the form of fiery tongues. The meaning of this event was demonstrated in the Apostle's miraculous ability to preach to the assembled crowds assembled, each in his own language. (Acts 2:1 and following)

The feast of Pentecost, then, is primarily a celebration of the third Person of the Trinity, the Holy Spirit, and demonstrates His importance for Christians called to be the ongoing Presence of the Incarnate God in history.

To understand what it means to be Pentecostal Christians (in the general sense of that word), though, it is worth noting that the first Pentecost took place during the Jewish feast of Shavuot, which commemorates Moses' giving of the law on Mount Sinai. Shavuot is also a festival for the harvest of grain and fruit. During this time, houses and synagogues are decorated with greenery, to celebrate the bounty of the earth.

(By the way, this is also a custom in many Orthodox churches, where Pentecost is known as the "Green Feast": the priest wears green vestments and the Church temple is decorated with greenery, following the Jewish tradition.)

The feast of Shavuot therefore celebrates spiritual completion and fruition. Just as the fruit of the earth comes to its fullness, so too the people of Israel, having obeyed and followed the almighty YHWH out of bondage in Egypt, finally receive the fruit of their sufferings: God's own words written by Moses on stone tablets.

The giving of the law raised a question, however: how could legal texts written on stone be translated into the inward convictions of individual believers? Something more was needed. God's words needed a spirit—literally, a *breath* (spirit means 'breath') to carry their meaning into a deeper place in the human heart.

149

In the Old Testament, God Himself gave or put His spirit (known in Hebrew as *ruah*) into specific people, such as prophets like Ezekiel, Isaiah and Jeremiah. The purpose of these anointed individuals was to demonstrate what it meant to live with an inward conviction and zeal for God's written law. Spirit-filled men and women in the Old Testament were sent to remind the people of Israel of the inner meaning of the law: that they were God's own people, called to love and serve Him with all their heart and soul and might.

And yet that was not enough. It was not enough to have only certain select people receive God's 'breath' and bear His word to the hearts of His people. Moses himself cried, *"Would that all the LORD's people were prophets, that the LORD would put his spirit upon them!"* (Numbers 11:29) Later, through Ezekiel, God promised to fulfill Moses' desire: *And I will put my spirit within you, and cause you to walk in my statutes and be careful to observe my ordinances. You shall dwell in the land which I gave to your fathers; and you shall be my people, and I will be your God.* (Ezekiel 36:27-28)

It was this Old Testament expectation—the hope that everyone could receive God's *ruah* and become bearers of His Word—that came to fruition at Pentecost. The fulfillment of Mosaic law, the embodiment of God's Word in the flesh, and the ultimate bearer of His spirit—Jesus Christ—made it possible for all men and women to receive the same Holy Spirit and become living, breathing "words of God' to the world.

When the Apostles spoke in many languages at Pentecost, it was the first sign that the knowledge of God through Jesus Christ was accessible to all through the Holy Spirit. The other "gifts of the Spirit," such as prophesy, angelic tongues, miracles, and discernment of spirits (see 1 Corinthians 12-14) were further signs that human beings could become "partakers of divine nature" (2 Peter 1:4). Such godlike gifts, though, were never ends in themselves, and ultimately Saint Paul challenges Christians to outgrow those lesser signs by loving each other with the self-emptying love of a God who Himself *is* love. (See 1 Cor. 12:31-13:13 and 1 John 4:8) Such love is the greatest sign of a mature Pentecostal Christian.

In addition, although Christians may know and name the Pentecostal spirit personally as the Holy Spirit, the Comforter sent by Christ from God, we by no means have exclusive possession of Him. After

150

all, the God who was crucified in the flesh also created the world by His Spirit "moving on the face of the waters." (Gen. 1:2) In that sense, the Spirit dwells in all peoples, in all times and cultures. As Saint Paul said to the philosophers of Athens, *"He is not far from each one of us, for `In him we live and move and have our being'; as even some of your poets have said, `For we are indeed his offspring.'"* (Acts 17:23, 27-28)

As I read those words, I recall the ancient Hindu greeting "Namaste" (Namas-teh), which means literally "I greet the god in you." As a Christian, I understand this not in a pantheistic fashion, but as reflecting the timeless intuition that each of us—Christian or not—is a bearer of God's Spirit, and each embodies His Word in unique and personal (though not always conscious) ways. In recognition of that astounding reality, I share with you an Eastern Orthodox prayer to the Holy Spirit: "O Heavenly King, the Comforter, the Spirit of Truth, everywhere present and filling all things, Treasury of blessings and Giver of life: come and abide in us, cleanse us from every impurity and save our souls, O Good One."

June 2009

The Journey Home

This past week marked the beginning of Great Lent, a period in which Christians all over the world prepare themselves to celebrate the Cross and Resurrection of Christ at Easter.

Although Orthodox Christians follow slightly different traditions around Great Lent, the basic meaning of these forty days is the same for us. To put it simply, Lent is a journey back to our spiritual home in the Presence of God, who created us so that He might embrace us and love us, and that we might love Him in return.

The Incarnation of Jesus Christ is the fulfilment of God's love for us, for in Him God took human nature to Himself once and for all, making it a part of who He is. And in the Passion of Christ — His suffering on the Cross, death and resurrection — the divine-human union was completed. God had finally unite Himself with human experience, from birth to death and beyond.

Our realization of this astounding and mysterious Fact is the purpose of Great Lent, which is in no way isolated from the rest of the year. Lent, rather, is a kind of temporal magnifying glass, revealing in intense, close-up detail the meaning not only of the rest of the year, but the rest of our lives. The coming forty days remind us more potently and poignantly than ever of our calling to continuously return to God's Presence. He has united Himself to us, and we must unite ourselves to Him daily, moment by moment.

Nowhere is this journey of reunion more perfectly described than in Jesus' Parable of the Prodigal Son. Many of you may know the story, which is told in the fifteenth chapter of St. Luke's Gospel. A young man, perhaps fed up with the tedium and restrictions of life at home, demands his father give him an advance on his inheritance. The son then goes into the world and blows the cash on "fast cars, faster women and recreational chemicals." Predictably, the money runs out and when a famine strikes, the young man is left destitute and starving. He finally hits bottom, working for a pig farmer (the most distasteful kind of job for a pious Jew) and worse yet, yearning for the pigs' food.

The image of the Prodigal Son, sitting miserably in the pig pen while he yearns for the slop, coming to himself as he remembers his father's household (Luke 15:17), then rising and going back home (Luke 15:20), illustrate precisely the steps we take as human beings in our return to God. Let's take them in order of the parable.

Having spent all our resources trying to master our own destinies, we hit bottom. Perhaps we get sick unexpectedly. Perhaps we lose a job. Perhaps some unexpected event impinges on our lives—a downturn in the economy, for instance... Regardless of the specifics, we find ourselves deprived of the ability to control our circumstances.

Sooner or later (and more often later than sooner, unfortunately), we come to recognize the need for aid beyond ourselves. We perceive within ourselves a hunger for something beyond the slop to which we have become accustomed.

The philosopher Charles Taylor describes this experience of longing in his book *The Secular Age*: "[it is] a distance, an absence, an exile, a seemingly irremediable incapacity ever to reach this place; an absence of power, a confusion.... We lose a sense of where the place of fullness is, even of what fullness could consist in, we feel we've forgotten what it would look like, or cannot believe in it anymore. But the misery of absence, of loss, is still there, indeed, it is in some ways even more acute."

Having recognized our need for that "absent something" beyond ourselves—defined as "God"—we embark upon a process of bringing ourselves and our lives in all their brokenness back to Him. In Christian tradition, this is known as *repentance*, which is not merely feeling bad for our sins, but the continual act of returning our hearts and minds back to the One who is the source of our lives. This self-offering back to God begins in prayer and is sealed in the giving of ourselves to one another through concrete acts of love and service. In short, we commit to living as a servant in our father's household.

This then is the lifelong human journey back to God, symbolized in the Parable of the Prodigal Son and highlighted in the period of Lent. And whether you celebrate the next forty days liturgically or not, it is certainly an appropriate time to explore for yourselves a simple question: "Where do I stand in this journey?"

If you are still partying with a pocketful of cash like the Prodigal Son in his heyday, consider that the party may end in the pig pen. If you have hit bottom and are sitting in the pig pen, consider the possibility of a better life beyond what you can attain for yourself. And if you are already on the way home, rehearsing your speech of repentance, consider that your Father may have been watching for you since you left, and is even now waiting to embrace you without conditions or expectations, waiting to put the ring of His authority on your finger and feed you with the food of joy, peace and eternal life.

Wherever you find yourself on the journey back to God this year, now is the time to come home.

February 2010

Saint Mary of Egypt

In the Eastern Orthodox tradition, the fifth Sunday of Great Lent is devoted to the memory of a woman who stands as an example, not just of what it means to be a Christian, but what it means to be a human being.

She is known to us only as Mary. Born and raised in Egypt in the fifth century, she ran away at the age of 12 to the big city of Alexandria, where she lived on the street, begging or spinning flax for a living while she engaged in a life of sexual debauchery. As Mary makes clear in the account of her life, it was not as if she was living a life of prostitution in order to survive. "It was not for the sake of gain..." she says. "Often when they wished to pay me, I refused the money. I acted in this way so as to make as many men as possible to try to obtain me, doing free of charge what gave me pleasure."

These details alone are disturbing. Consider the horrific realities of child prostitution, then take away the external forces of oppression and exploitation, and imagine a child so emotionally and psychologically damaged that she would *willingly* allow herself to be abused by whoever wished it. It hardly bears thinking about...

According to her own testimony—witnessed by a priest named Zosimas and later recorded by Sophronius, Patriarch of Jerusalem—Mary lived in this manner for seventeen years. Then, one summer's day, she was seized by a whim to follow a group of pilgrims who were traveling to the Holy Land. When they arrived in Jerusalem and entered a local church, Mary attempted to follow, but found herself physically unable to do so, "as if there was a detachment of soldiers standing there to oppose my entrance."

After trying several times to enter and failing, Mary had an epiphany. "The word of salvation gently touched the eyes of my heart," she says, "and revealed to me that it was my unclean life which barred the entrance to me. I began to weep and lament and beat my breast, and to sigh from the depths of my heart."

Following this revelation, Mary experienced a conversion and devoted her life to Christ. She departed from Alexandria, crossed the Jordan River, and spent the next 47 years living in the wilderness. Only then did the priest Zosimas discovered her, now in her seventies and completely naked, her clothes having rotted off her body.

The account relates miracles associated with Mary. According to Zosimas' witness, she knew his name without being introduced to him; when she prayed, she levitated off the ground; she walked on the water to cross the Jordan River and receive the Eucharist from him; she was miraculously transported to the place where she died; and a lion came out of the desert, tame as a pet dog, to dig her grave.

All of this is to say that after a lifetime of struggle, Saint Mary of Egypt found freedom from the horrific psychological and spiritual forces that sought to destroy her, attaining the ultimate destiny of a human being, which is to become a partaker of divine nature. (see 2 Peter 1:4). From unfathomable depths of abasement, she rose to immense heights of faith. The readings prescribed for her in the liturgy of the Orthodox Church compare her to the woman who wept at Jesus' feet, about whom He says, "I tell you, her sins, which are many, are forgiven, for she loved much; but he who is forgiven little, loves little." (Luke 7:47)

What does the life of this obscure Egyptian woman in the fifth century have to say to us?

So often we are told that God loves and favours us more the more righteous we become. Saint Mary's story reminds us that there are no depths to which we can descend where God will not meet and embrace us. Indeed, I would suggest that the more debased we are, the greater is God's rejoicing when we turn to Him in faith. While God does love everyone equally, He surely has a special place for the weakest and most miserable members of the human race who seek His help. I am convinced His love is somehow more *intense*, more urgent, the closer to the bottom He finds us when we turn to Him.

But what if we are not one of those "fortunate unfortunates"? What if we have not hit a bottom anywhere near as low Saint Mary's?

For us ordinary sinners, our task lies in realizing the abyss of our indifference and cold-heartedness, the expanse of our wilful ignorance to God's goodness and generosity, the height of our hubris and self-deceit. Our real challenge consists in honesty, pushing hard to see the truth of our lives, just as St. Mary pushed to get into the church.

If we push hard enough and long enough, the answers will come. They may not be answers we like; the vision of our brokenness is likely to be as horrific for us as it was for Saint Mary. Still, if we can bear the face that truth, as she was willing to do, we will discover just how much we have been forgiven. And when that happens, we will finally learn just how much God loves us, despite ourselves, and just how high our calling is to be His beloved children, partakers of His divine nature and heirs of His Kingdom.

March 2010

Saint Aidan of Lindisfarne

Two and a half years ago, a small group of Eastern Orthodox Christians known collectively as the East Kootenay Orthodox Christian Fellowship decided to adopt as their patron Saint Aidan, Bishop of Lindisfarne.

It was a radical decision in many respects. Though Aidan is a well-known English saint whose life falls within a period of jurisdictional and doctrinal unity of the eastern and western churches, he is not very familiar in Eastern Orthodox circles. In choosing the patronage of Saint Aidan, Orthodox Christians in the East Kootenay committed to building bridges between Christians, working towards healing the divisions that have torn us apart.

The choice of Saint Aidan, in the example of his life, also reflects the manner in which our community hopes to approach and interact with our neighbours in this region. In 634 A.D., the newly-converted Oswald attained the kingship of Northumbria (northern England) and embarked on a process of bringing his people to Christianity. He at first summoned a Bishop named Corman from the great monastery of Iona. Corman came but had little success with the people, who rejected him out of hand.

Returning to Iona, he complained bitterly that the pagans were too hard-hearted to receive the Gospel. Aidan, who was a monk at Iona at this time, spoke up, saying: "Brother, it seems to me that you were too severe with your ignorant hearers. You should have followed the example of the apostles, who began by giving people the milk of simple teaching, gradually nourishing them with the Word of God until they were capable of greater perfection, and so could follow the more demanding precepts of Christ."

Recognizing the heart of a pastor in Aidan, the monks of Iona immediately put him forward as the next candidate to evangelize the Northumbrians. Aidan was later ordained Bishop, choosing the island of Lindisfarne as the seat of his diocese. The island was ideal for a man who was both a pastor and a monk. When the tide was in, the sea made Aidan's headquarters inaccessible and ideal for the quiet solitude of prayer. When the tide went out, however, people could walk easily across the sandbar to meet with him.

Aidan was unlike most Bishops of his day. Noblemen and Church authorities were expected to ride horses everywhere as a sign of their power and superior status, but Aidan chose to walk everywhere he went, conversing politely with the people and slowly interesting them in Christianity. Once, King Oswin (Oswald's successor) gave Aidan a fine horse, but Aidan sold it and gave the money to the first beggar he met. This was how he operated generally, using tithes and donations only for what he and his monks needed, then giving away the rest to the poor and needy of the earth.

There is no doubt that Saint Aidan was a man of prayer, who loved and studied the Scriptures as the wellspring of his faith. Wherever he travelled, he set up his living quarters beside the local church, where "a tent was erected for him against one of its wooden buttresses. Aidan could thus lean against the buttress, praying." And this, it is said, is how Aidan died, standing in prayer, leaning against the buttress of the Church.

No doubt many of us have encountered Christians and Christian leaders like Corman, the first candidate sent to Northumbria: severe, rigid, extreme and judgmental. Saint Aidan offers a different vision of how Christians are to bear witness to those around them. Through gentleness, by meeting people where they are, by living a life of quiet devotion to prayer and study of the Scriptures, the community that seeks the prayers of Saint Aidan also hopes to share in his unique example of Christ's love for all of God's children.

August 2008

159

Signposts on the Daily Walk

A Work in Progress

My neighbour is building a house. Though still a few months away from completion (I am not sure if the plumbing is in yet), it will be one day be a nice little building, well-constructed and comfortable.

Imagine, though, if a passerby stopped to look at the current structure and exclaimed, "What an ugly house! It doesn't even have doors and the walls aren't painted. And where on earth are the front steps?"

Would we not look askance at such a reaction? We might even rebuke that foolish person for judging the house before it is completed. And yet, when it comes to other people, we regularly indulge in such pre-judgments.

Why is that? Let me answer the question with another question: have you ever reconnected with a childhood friend after many years? This happened to me a few years ago on Facebook. Reunited with a girl I knew when I lived in Zimbabwe, I was astonished to discover that she had grown up, gotten married, had children, and now works at Barney's of New York.

Imagine that! People have lives outside of our experience of them! It seems obvious, but for me it was a revelation, because in my mind, my friend had been frozen in time. Until I encountered her again, she was a perpetual twelve-year-old and the object of my boyish taunts and affections. Now she is a woman, with a lifetime of adult experiences and fond memories, only a few of which involve me...

Such is life in a fallen world, where we are each the centre of our own little universe. When someone enters our orbit, we assume that everything we happen to learn of them is all there is to know. After all, what else can there be beyond ourselves? Surely the world ends beyond my horizons!

It takes a great effort on our parts (or at least, on my part) to realize that there are dimensions of other people's lives that predate me, and that will survive me. There are depths I will never know and most importantly of all, processes of development and growth that are invisible to me.

When we encounter someone, we are meeting them along the way somewhere. If a person rubs us the wrong way, commits some *faux pas*, or is just a jerk, it is too easy for us to judge that action as if came from a finished person, rather than from someone who is really a work in progress.

As a Christian, I believe that salvation was God's act completed "once for all" with the Incarnation of Jesus Christ. However, I also believe that we must cooperate with God's activity if we are going participate in what He has done. Salvation is not something God forces on us; we must also accept it, as Mary did when she said, "Let it be to me according to Your word."

Our cooperation with God's will is a daily challenge and involves choices we make to love Him and our neighbour moment by moment. Quite simply, we are not perfect yet, but if we choose to cooperate with God's action, we are being perfected daily. As the Apostle Paul puts it, "Though our outer nature is wasting away, our inner nature is being renewed every day." (2 Cor. 4:16)

In this process, God uses other people as His primary instruments. An abrasive encounter, an altercation, a struggle, an argument—in all these events He shapes me and others into the people He created us to be.

How do we evaluate the ultimate value of these encounters for us? Quite simply, we don't. Heisenberg's Uncertainty Principle says that is impossible to know both the position and the velocity of a subatomic particle, because the light we use to take the measurement affects the particle's movement.

The same may well be said about our daily relations with others. There is simply no accurate way to judge the ultimate significance of any personal encounter in my life, no matter how small. I cannot see where someone has been, nor can I determine precisely where they will go as a result of our meeting.

163

All I can do in the end is go easy on every person I encounter, recognizing that he or she is God's house, still under construction. Work has been done that I do not know of, and work still needs to be done before a final judgment can be pronounced. To judge them now would look as ridiculous as someone criticizing my neighbour's half-built house before it was finished.

On the other side of this warning, however, is a hopeful message. If our relationships are broken now, if people are insensitive, unkind, cruel, judgmental or selfish now, they may not be so forever. Though they may not change today, tomorrow, or even in our lifetimes, we can be assured that they are not finished yet. They are still in the hands of their loving Creator, who subjects them to the hammer and nail and saw in this life, in the hope that one day they will stand completed, the perfected masterwork of the Great Craftsman. We can find hope and even joy in that today.

April 2010

Found in Translation

Several days ago, my wife and I were having a "disagreement" on the subject of Christmas trees. I won't bore you with the details, except to say that after several minutes of bickering, we came to realize that the source of our enmity lay in our differing understandings of what the phrase "Christmas tree" actually meant.

By this I do not mean that we were fighting about the dictionary definition of "Christmas tree" i.e. a tree of the evergreen variety, traditionally decorated and kept in the house or public places around December 25th.

No, our problem did not lie with the surface meaning of the phrase "Christmas tree," but rather with its deeper associations.

You see, when my wife thinks of "Christmas tree," she remembers those special days of childhood and youth when her family would drive out into the woods, cut down a 15 foot Noble fir, bring it home and decorate it to the accompaniment of Christmas carols, hot apple cider and cookies.

By contrast, I am not greatly inspired by Christmas trees. I grew up on the Equator, where evergreens are non-existent. We never even had a real tree, let alone go out to cut one down. Our trees were decorated, but decorating them was just a practical task that someone accomplished at some point before Christmas.

For my beloved Jaime, "Christmas tree" is the embodiment of family, comfort, and joy. When I hear the same words, I think of a necessary object to be acquired and decorated by whatever means is most convenient.

No wonder, then, that my wife and I fought over the importance of Christmas trees. Although we were using the same words, we were actually speaking two different languages. Superficially identical, my wife's "Christmas tree" and my "Christmas tree" referred to two profoundly different and opposed realities.

If you think about it, this petty domestic squabble points to a core problem in much of human life. How many national, political or social conflicts have erupted when groups use identical words — like "freedom," "democracy" and "human rights" — in contradictory ways, all the while insisting that their definition is correct?

How often have we traded common words like "family," "friendship," or "love," only to be hurt when others don't seem to understand us?

As a pastor, I am only too aware of just how loaded are words like "father," "righteousness," "God," "obedience" and "authority" in the lives of those to whom I minister. And as an Eastern Orthodox priest, I am often bemused at western Christian arguments over "faith" versus "works" and "Scripture" versus "tradition" — words that are superficially familiar to me, but whose definitions I do not share.

Whether in the realm of the national, the personal or the spiritual, the problem is the same: translation. People use words and as long as these words appear to mean the same things, they assume that they are communicating.

It just isn't so.

Like my marital disagreement over Christmas trees, the problem lies in the deeper meanings. If people say, "We are fighting for freedom!" do they mean, "We are fighting so that your people can have the freedom to choose between Nike and Reebok," or "We are fighting so that our right believing people can be free to worship Allah in a proper manner"?

If someone says, "I love you," are they referring to a warm and intense emotion that can flicker and fade away in time, or a lifetime commitment to give themselves to another person, regardless of emotions?

If someone says, "We are saved by faith," are they referring to a crucial moment in which we recognize certain propositions about God and His love in Jesus Christ, or a series of faithful choices, each of which brings us closer or pushes us further away from God? Or is it something in between?

You can see how so many conflicts come to be. Most of us don't really ask ourselves what someone else means by the words they use. We just see common vocabulary and plough ahead, assuming that our definition is the one the other person is using, or worse yet, that our definition is right and theirs is wrong.

The answer to this pervasive failing in our human character lies in proper translation. By this I don't mean better or more accurate dictionaries. I mean taking the time to understand what each person really means by the words they use.

As a husband, recognizing my wife's associations with the phrase "Christmas tree" went a long way to healing the rift between us. As a pastor, recognizing the emotional and spiritual baggage that many people bring to the Church has been crucial to helping them find a true reconciliation with God.

Seeking and discovering these inner meanings takes time. It involves humility, openness and commitment. It is often painful and frustrating. It requires us to gain trust, which is reluctantly given and easily betrayed.

As difficult as this process is, however, it must be undertaken. We must make the effort to fully translate the meanings of each other's words, spiritually, personally, culturally. If we don't, we may be doomed to continue talking at without understanding each other, much less achieving anything like unity or agreement.

November 2010

The Instinct for Greatness

I would like to end the year by sharing with you a personal spiritual struggle that may be of general interest.

Throughout my adult life I have often faced the urge to strive for and achieve some kind of "greatness." In my teens, I wanted to be a great mathematician or cosmologist like Ramanujan, Einstein or Stephen Hawking.

In my twenties, I wanted to be a great poet along the lines of Dylan Thomas, T.S. Eliot, W.B. Yeats, or Rainer Maria Rilke. Then I sought to be a great writer of prose, taking as my idols Gabriel Garcia Marquez, Hemingway, and Steinbeck.

Some of my efforts paid off: poems and short stories published in journals, and eventually a young adult novel called *The Nightmare Tree*. And of course, I continue to write articles for the local newspaper...

Still, these modest rewards weren't enough. I still wanted to be "great." You know, really *great*, with my name sitting on "Top 10" lists for generations to come. Poet, writer, preacher, teacher, pastor, father, husband — it didn't matter what "Top 10" list it was, so long as I was on it, somewhere near the top...

It sounds silly and prideful, and it is. I think, though, that within each of us resides a similar impulse to greatness. Deep down, we all want to know that we are fulfilling our potential. We all want to be told that we are doing a *great* job. At the root of our being, we all desire to be valued in a way that is distinct from others.

Time and experience often erode our impulse to greatness, or sour it into bitterness and a kind of resigned mediocrity. Somewhere deep inside, though, I believe that the urge remains in some form or another, and an important task in the spiritual life involves accounting for it and addressing it in some way.

But how?

It is my belief that every human impulse is rooted something good and pure that is often used for an unnatural purpose. As the fulfillment of love, sex is good, but it is easily twisted using others for selfish ends. Enjoying food is good but when overindulged, it easily slips into gluttony. The thirst for justice and indignation at injustice can easily be perverted to judge, condemn and even harm other people.

In a similar way, the impulse to greatness lies in a natural and good desire to become the human beings we were created to be. A 7th century Christian teacher called Maximus taught that when God created us, He did so with a "logos" or idea of our potential in life. This idea is rooted in God's ultimate "Logos," His ultimate "Idea" for the ideal human life—Jesus Christ, who is the final and definitive "Word of God" made flesh.

Maximus' theology is complex, but the short of it is that when we live out our lives in obedience to the ultimate pattern that God has provided in Jesus Christ, we also fulfill our own particular pattern of existence. To put it simply, we become an expression of Jesus Christ in our own unique and particular personalities and ways. We each become a singular "word" that speaks *the* Word—Jesus Christ—in our own lives.

In that light, my impulse to greatness is really the impulse to fulfill God's "idea" of who He created me to be. What I really want in the end is for every aspect of my life to fully and completely "speak" the Word of God—Jesus Christ—to the world, using a "word" that is uniquely mine *and no one else's.*

Knowing this, however, the question remains: how can I attain this goal? The answer is simpler than you might think: I don't need to *do* anything, because everything has been accomplished. God has already given Himself in Christ, and in baptism, we have become "a letter from Christ … written not with ink but with the Spirit of the living God, not on tablets of stone but on tablets of human hearts." (2 Cor. 3:3)

The person that I was created to be has already been born. By grace, I have everything I need to be complete, fulfilled and perfected, and now my only task is to allow God to feed and nurture that embryonic person day by day "to mature manhood, to the measure of the stature of the fulness of Christ." (Eph. 4:13)

This is an inward effort, not an outward one. Being a "great" human being doesn't mean excelling in the realms of science, art, literature, theology, parenting or whatever. Being a "great" human being does not mean being a great achiever in the world and receiving applause from our fellow human beings. That inclination is just a twisted version of the true impulse to greatness, which is the desire to live in complete acceptance of the life God has given us, and to be content with *His* praise alone.

My goal in the New Year, then, is simple: to strive for true greatness by becoming more present with whatever and whoever He gives me in each moment. The more I accept what He gives, the more I allow myself to be shaped by what He gives into the "word" that He wants me to be, the greater I become. It's that simple.

If my efforts result in less than perfect worldly "achievements," because I was more concerned with the person or situation in front of me, rather than with crafting some article or sermon to perfection, so be it. Just as Jesus Himself had "no beauty that we should desire Him," (Is. 53:2) a life perfected in His image and likeness need not be externally glorious. I ask you to pray that I learn that lesson in 2010, even as I pray that you too would accept whatever God gives in the coming year and fulfil your deepest impulse to be made as perfect as He is.

December 2009

Living in the "Same Old"

Perform a little thought experiment with me, if you would. Think back over the past five months, from the New Year until the present, and ask yourself how many days you would characterize as exciting, extraordinary, or life-altering.

Having trouble? As hard I could, I could count no more than five days that come anywhere close to meeting the above criteria. Five days out of about 150—that's just over 3%. In this, I don't think I'm really unique. For most of us, 99% of life consists of the mundane, the ordinary, and the plain old dull. We get up, go to work, take care of family stuff, play, watch TV, eat, go on the Internet, go to bed, get up...

The rituals of daily, weekly, monthly, and yearly existence are relatively conventional for all of us: births and birthdays, weddings, funerals, graduations, medical appointments, and so on. As human beings, we share this common heritage of customs, ceremonies, and common experiences that bind us together. The "spikes"—unusual or unique events that distinguish us and change our lives—are few and far between.

This reality stands in sharp contrast with human life as it is often portrayed in movies, literature (especially the escapist kind), internet and television. The media by its very nature depicts the high points and the low points of life, often within the span of minutes, not hours. For the most part, the pervasive ordinariness that we all know is glossed over or ignored in favour of the most glamorous or dolorous moments.

If we spend a lot of time consuming media in all its different varieties, we may be tempted into thinking that life should be the way the media portrays it. I remember a comedy sketch I recently heard in which the comedian lamented that he couldn't say, as characters did in the movies, that he would "be on the next flight out" whenever he wanted to. He was stuck instead looking for the

171

best deals online, and managing all of the frustrating little travel details that movie characters never seem to have to deal with.

The problems start when we come to believe that the life depicted in the media is somehow attainable in the real world. We start to think that the mundane quality of our lives are unusual, perhaps reflecting some defect in ourselves, whether it is a lack of money or a lack of character. Our dissatisfaction drives us to seek out more and more wealth and material possessions. Our unhappiness drives us to fill our lives with "highs" in the form of constant entertainment, thrill-seeking, sex, alcohol or drugs…

When we give in to the media's deceit, the vast bulk of our daily routines can become a burden to us. We can't wait for the weekend, when we can inject a little excitement into our existence. We live for the excitement, while a pall falls over the rest of our days, which must be merely endured until the next high arrives.

I think we can all agree that this is no way to live. The question is, how can we stop merely putting up with the "same old" and start actually finding value in it? The first step, I think, is to remind ourselves that media reality does not and cannot correspond one-to-one with real human life. No one on the planet, even the most wealthy and powerful, live exactly as the movies would portray them. Sex is never accompanied by an orchestra, and no one ever just jumps on the next flight to wherever they want to go. Even Bill Gates has to wait for clearance before taking off in his private jet…

We need to stop denying that life is vastly ordinary and mostly pretty dull. Let's get that through our heads by spending a little less time listening to the voices and watching the images that try to tell us otherwise.

Secondly, we need to realize that routine, ritual, and repetition are processes inherent to human life. God built a whole lot of "same old" into our lives for a reason. We seem to need those times to percolate, marinate, and generally soak in the more intense moments of our existence. We seem to understand deep experiences best by having a period to consider and reflect upon them in long, uninterrupted stretches.

Take marriage, for instance. The intensity and excitement of the engagement, the wedding, the honeymoon, the early months, and even the birth of the first child, require years of quiet routine and habit to find their true meaning in our lives. There is certainly excitement to be found throughout the life of a marriage; my point is that the true significance of a marriage does not become fully evident without those times in which nothing much happens, or else in which the same thing happens over and over again.

The "same old" exists to teach us the deeper meaning of life. Don't ask me why; it just seems to be the way we were built.

Finally, we need to see the ordinariness of life as a challenge to look deeper and discover the extraordinary. Jesus commands us to avoid "vain repetitions," but in life—as in prayer—repetition is only vain if we are not really paying attention. The solution to vain repetitions—both in life and prayer—is simply an attitude of greater attentiveness to that which we would otherwise ignore.

The "same old"—those flat, occasionally undulating plains of existence—call us to look at mundane things like clouds and sunsets, to smell the coming rain, to touch a new leaf and taste a cherry, and discover again what Gerard Manley Hopkins called "the dearest freshness deep down things." The ordinary, repetitive sounds of life—the rush of traffic, the creak of the house, a bird singing, the wind in the trees—call us to delve deeper and really hear the "still, small voice" that speaks to us of eternity.

May 2010

Looking for Love (in All the Wrong Places)

I recently heard someone confess a struggle that I (and I would suspect, others) know very well. He said, "For years, my sense of self worth has depended on two things: my achievements, and the opinions of others."

How true that has been in my life! Because I am the sort of person who generally does well at whatever he puts his hand to, I am particularly susceptible to equating my value as a human being with the result of any given activity.

The problem with this approach, of course, is that it is a *floating* measure. When things "go well" for us (however that success is measured), then we are buoyed upward on a tide of euphoria. Life is beautiful and God loves us.

When, however, things fall apart (or seem to), when glitches, stumbles, hiccups and hesitations happen, then our self-worth shrinks or collapses. Darkness comes over. God seems far away and we ask why He is punishing us.

Caught up in this habit, we easily fall prey to perfectionism — it has to be just right, or there must be something wrong with us. Or perhaps we tend towards procrastination — if there is a chance the result of our effort is not going to be perfect, we just won't do it, or else we'll put it off for another time.

Whether we tend towards perfectionism or procrastination, though, the drive to define ourselves by what we accomplish or fail to accomplish is a circular rollercoaster ride, with dizzying highs and crashing lows.

The impulse to measure ourselves by the opinions of others creates a similar pattern. When we are showered with gratitude, praise and attention, we feel loved, valued and confident. When, however, people disagree with us, get upset with us, are indifferent to us, or seem to take us for granted, we are tempted to feel less than worthwhile.

If a life governed by achievement is a roller coaster, a life dependent on the opinions of others is a game whose objective is to extract the necessary number of ego strokes from our children, our spouse, our friends and coworkers. This is done either by subtle forms of manipulation, or else by engaging in "people pleasing" techniques. And then there are those who define themselves in *negative* terms, and therefore seek negative and even abusive attention to maintain their degraded self-image.

Whatever the case, maintaining our self-esteem through the opinions of others leads us to use everyone we encounter as vehicles to our selfish ends, thus depriving our relationships of their humanity.

Is there another option? After all, doesn't everyone need to feel appreciated, approved of, loved and valued? Where else can we find such affirmation of our worth, if not in our accomplishments, or in the people around us?

In his second Epistle to the Corinthians, the Apostle Paul offers us a personal answer to that question. Having told his hearers about certain mystical visions and revelations he received from God (2 Cor. 12:3-4), he says that "to keep me from being too elated by the abundance of revelations, a thorn was given me in the flesh, a messenger of Satan, to harass me, to keep me from being too elated." (2 Cor. 12:7) Paul asked God three time to take this "thorn in the flesh" away from him, but God's only response was, "My grace is sufficient for you, for my power is made perfect in weakness." (2 Cor. 12:9)

The Apostle confesses that he wanted his spiritual achievements and the approbation of others to determine his sense of well-being. However, his personal struggle (no one knows what it was) sabotaged his best efforts. In the end, he realized that God had given him a specific weakness precisely so that he would not depend on human avenues to affirm his worth. Ultimately, his "boast" could only be in the One who had created him, who had invested him with intrinsic value from his mother's womb, and who had suffered in the flesh in order to restore him and the rest of the humanity to its intended glory.

As the world compels us to seek fame, honour and glory, striving to be a "great" this or a "famous" that, the Gospel challenges us to realize that such desires are actually misguided expressions of a more basic impulse: the need to know that God loves us. When we seek affirmation through our achievements or the opinions of others, we are really looking for God's love in all the wrong places.

When, therefore, I am tempted to live as if my self-worth depends on whatever I accomplish or what others think of me, I need instead to boast "of the things that show my weakness," (2 Cor. 11:30) which is to say, I need to face my frail humanity. I need to buck the overwhelming temptation to feed my ego, and instead cry out like a helpless child. Only then can I open the door that allows God to lift me up, embrace me, and tell me that He loves me. Only then can I find in Him my true worth and value, as His beloved child, a partaker in His divine nature, a son and heir of His kingdom.

October 2009

Love, or Indulgence?

As Canadians, we pride ourselves on loving our neighbours. Canada's social policies, our comprehensive welfare system, our hallowed universal health care, our traditional military stance as peacekeepers—all of these national initiatives represent a secular version of the social Gospel rooted in Jesus' commandment feed the hungry, clothe the naked, visit those who are imprisoned, and generally care for those less fortunate than ourselves. (Matthew 25:31-46)

The impulse to minister to the poor, the sick, and the oppressed is an inalienable part of the Canadian soul. Even such apparently contradictory decisions to apologize to the First Nations for cultural genocide while honouring Henry Morgentaler with the Order of Canada, in fact represent two sides of the same motivation: to avoid causing grief or harm to people we perceive as marginalized in some way.

This, then, is Canadian love. The question is, is it *Christian* love? For us, love is often an emotional reality. If I feel good about myself, then I am loving myself. If I make you feel good about yourself, I am loving *you*. Even if I don't agree with you, as long as your feel-good activities don't impinge on mine, I am prepared to "affirm" what you do, because that's what we think love is. In reality, however, our impulse to "love" usually translates as: "Do what you want where I'm not directly affected, and we'll all be happy."

Frankly, this is not love in the scriptural and Christian sense of that word. Let's take a basic verse: "For God so loved the world that he gave his only Son, that whoever believes in him should not perish but have eternal life." (John 3:16) You've probably heard it before, but read it again carefully. Love is primarily God's impulse to give *life* to the world.

And what is "life" in the scriptural sense? For the people of the ancient Near East, the answer was very concrete. Life was an oasis of drinkable water in the desert. It was food in times of drought and famine. Life was about *survival*, not good feelings. And love was about seeking to preserve someone's life at all costs, no matter how *bad* it made them feel in the short run. So John 3:16 is really saying simply that God is quite happy to hurt both His and our feelings in the short run so that we can *survive* in the "long run," which is to say, *forever*.

As a father of three small children, I have learned this truth in very practical ways. When I discovered my two-year-old son running around the house with a pointed end of a pair of scissors in his mouth, I did not hesitate upset him on the spot in order to remind him that such activity is life-threatening. That's how I love my children: by seeking their life, their survival, both physical, mental, spiritual—no matter how badly they may feel about it at any given moment. To do otherwise is not to love them, but to *indulge* them. And however pleasant indulgence may feel now, there's always a price to pay later...

If we call ourselves Christians and choose to live a faith rooted in the Scriptures, our most important imperative is to love one another. But what does love really mean? I cannot speak for Canadian society, but if we call ourselves disciples of Jesus Christ, we need to draw a clear distinction between love and indulgence. And then we need to make a courageous decision to seek life for ourselves and those within our sphere of influence, whatever may come of it. Be sensitive, wise and discreet, by all means, but in the end, don't pull punches. After all, when it comes to matters of survival, what's a few hurt feelings and bruised egos?

September 2008

"The Present Moment is Perfect"

I heard those words spoken a number of years ago by someone who suffered daily from a crippling addiction, and had every reason to feel otherwise about what the present moment might bring him. Witnessing this man overcome his addiction daily as result of his attitude was a watershed moment in my own spiritual journey. Since then "the present moment is perfect" has become a personal motto of mine, a reminder that I want to live my life in an attitude of total acceptance of whatever is now.

Living in the present moment is a theme we find across the geography of human spirituality. Buddhism and other Far Eastern religions hold the *now* as sacred. Modern spiritual writers like Eckhart Tolle and his popular book *The Power of Now* claim that the path to enlightenment and happiness begins and ends with the present moment. "Just for today" is the quintessential refrain in 12-Step program of Alcoholics Anonymous.

The question is, what makes the present moment—fleeting and ephemeral as it is—so powerful? Living for today seems to work, but why? I would suggest the answer flows from the central tenet of Christianity: the Incarnation.

The boldest and most radical claim of the Christian faith is that the eternal and transcendent God, was born, lived and died as a ordinary human being. Yahweh, the God who is without beginning and end, who cannot be contained, allowed Himself to be contained in the four-dimensional framework of life in this world.

And where does life in this world actually take place except in the present moment? Much as we would like to turn back the hands of time or penetrate the mists of the future, our consciousness can only act within the boundaries of the now. Such is the reality of being created beings, unable (by own efforts at least) to transcend the space-time continuum.

In the Christian view, then, God (with all that the word 'God' implies) enters human life and is confined to the present moment. As a result, something remarkable happens. Eastern Orthodox theology refers to it as *communicatio idiomatum* — the exchange of properties. As God takes on human life in the present moment as a part of His identity in Christ, human life simultaneously acquires the potential to become divine.

The New Testament testifies to this startling implication of the Incarnation at the very outset of Jesus's ministry. The essence of Jesus' preaching is "Repent, for the kingdom of God is *at hand*" (Mark 1:15 and Matt. 4:17), which is to say that salvation is to be found here and now, in human life as it is expressed in the person of Jesus Himself. Saint Paul reiterates this powerful message when he tells his Corinthian hearers that "now is the acceptable time; behold, now is the day of salvation." (2 Cor. 6:2)

There is a further implication. If the eternal God entered human life and made it a part of Himself in Christ, then human life is an inextricable part of God's eternal nature. And if this same eternal God, who joined human nature to Himself at a particular moment in history, also created the world in His image and likeness (Gen. 1:26), then it is no wonder that the sacredness of the present moment is inherent across cultures and religions, even those *prior* to the advent of Christianity. After all, it was He who joined Himself to the present moment, who also created the present moment in the first place!

The present moment is so powerful, then, because it is the very point where God meets us and makes it possible for us to become "partakers in divine nature." (2 Pet. 1:4) No wonder that living "just for today" is such a source of enlightenment and peace, not just for Christians, but for any human being who chooses to live his or her life that way.

But what about all the suffering we see in the present moment? What about the evils and injustices and horrors of Gaza city, the Congo and Zimbabwe that are happening *right now*? How can those present moments be perfect? The short answer is paradoxical: those moments are both wrong *and* perfect. How so? The central prayer of the Eastern Orthodox liturgy of Saint Basil offers a revealing petition to God: "preserve the good in goodness and make the evil to be good by Your goodness."

By joining human life and making it a part of who He is, God did not take away our pains, sorrows and sufferings. There still remains much that is wrong in the world. However, by His Incarnation, God did make it possible for us to offer up all that is broken in the world to Him, and in so doing, transform those things into a sacrifice of praise to Him. As the Psalmist says, "A sacrifice acceptable to God is broken spirit; a broken and contrite heart, O God, You will not despise." (Ps. 51:17)

What makes the present moment perfect, then, is not the absence tragedy or evil; rather, perfection is the act of offering up each moment, *whatever* it may contain, to God. Only then can the good be preserved and the evil be "made good" by fulfilling the very purpose for which everything exists: to praise and give thanks to the One who created each moment, who filled it with Himself, and who made it possible for us to enter into the now and discover there the doorway to the divine peace and joy of His Kingdom.

January 2009

The Professional Spirit

Suppose you were standing in line-up at McDonald's, and the person ahead of you started to lambast the little old lady who was about to take his order. The subject of his tirade? Not her service skills, but McDonald's business practices, the nutritional value of its food, and its contribution to the greenhouse effect.

Wouldn't you feel sorry for the poor employee? After all, she can hardly be held responsible for the McDonald's corporate sins. As a reasonable onlooker of this scene, you might well say, "Lay off, will you? She just works here!"

In the context of our secular life, "I just work here" can be used as an excuse not to take responsibility; it can be a reneging of citizenship, a refusal to have a stake in the life of your community. In the spiritual life, however, "I just work here" is essential to relating to God and one another in the proper spirit.

This spirit, which I can only describe as "professional," is well described in the "Big Book" of Alcoholics Anonymous:

We had a new Employer. Being all powerful, He provided what we needed, if we kept close to Him and performed His work well. Established on such a footing we became less and less interested in ourselves, our little plans and designs. More and more we became interested in seeing what we could contribute to life. As we felt new power flow in, as we enjoyed peace of mind, as we discovered we could face life successfully, as we became conscious of His presence, we began to lose our fear of today, tomorrow or the hereafter. We were reborn. (*Alcoholics Anonymous*, p.63)

For alcoholics who have based their entire lives on themselves and the needs of their egos, the refreshing solution is to live more *professionally*, that is, as if they were merely employees of the universal "Employer."

Spiritual professionalism gives birth to freedom. The McDonald's employee is responsible for providing the best service she can and doing her work well, but beyond that, she cannot be held responsible for McDonald's corporate vision.

Similarly, if I as a human being "work" for the heavenly Employer, I am truly liberated from the responsibility of guiding my own destiny. All I need to do is perform the Employer's work well, that is, be dedicated and faithful to whatever task is set in front of me. The rest I can happily leave in God's hands.

I believe that we could use more spiritual professionalism in our world. We are a society largely dedicated to the cult of personality. We value the larger-than-life men and women who stand above their fellow human beings in the realms of art, science, politics, and entertainment, regarding them as the ancient Greeks regarded their gods on Mount Olympus. And even when an accomplishment is clearly a group effort, our first impulse is to isolate and identify the individual genius on whom we heap our adulation.

Consider, for instance, Canada's hockey victory at the Olympics. Who could doubt that the gold medal was won by the entire team? And yet whose name resounded most loudly in the stadium that afternoon except that of Sidney Crosby? We might pay lip service to the team, but do we not worship Crosby as the current hockey god of Canada?

Whatever its value may be in the secular world, the cult of personality is the source of ultimate death and destruction in the spiritual life. The fall of Lucifer came directly as a result of his attempt to style himself as God's equal—his own cult of personality. Spiritually, our attempts to make the ego the centre of our lives is nothing less than an imitation of Satan's prototype, with the same destructive results.

One of my seminary professors once told me, "God is the only valid ego." Like it or not, this is the very definition of spiritual reality. In the end, only God can say, "I am," which is why pious Jews never spoke the Name of God (which means "I am") out loud, for fear that "I" might be applied to the speaker. Their point is well taken: God's personality is the only one worth building a cult around. The most everyone else can say is that we are His representatives, sent by Him and accountable to Him for everything.

As long as we go on building our own cults of personality, the burden of orchestrating our universe will continue to crush us, and we will continue to be victims of what recovering alcoholics call "self-will run riot."

Instead, I propose that we try looking at our lives more professionally, viewing the challenges of being parents and children, spouses and friends, colleagues and neighbours, as simply a part of our human job description. As long as we do our work well, when some equivalent of the irate customer comes along to lambast us for something beyond our control, we can just say, "This is not about me. I just work here."

The professional spirit does not mean we cannot be passionate, dedicated, involved and intimate with the realities of our lives—spiritual and material. It just means that ultimately, Someone else is sitting at head office, and His is the final word. Knowing that truth is the real secret to the freedom, peace and joy of a life reborn.

April 2010

Resentment

Several days ago, my wife and I fell into one of those silly little squabbles that are such a prominent feature of day-to-day married life. You know the kind of fight I am talking about: they are never about the meaning of life, the existence of God, or even the profound ethical implications of cloning. The most fights are rather about those *other* big issues: whether or not the toilet seat should be left up; whose dirty dishes those are; where the salt shaker should be kept. You get the point.

These petty quarrels unleash what I consider the deadliest poison in any human relationship: resentment. Take my recent conflict, for instance. Something was left out and not returned to where it belonged. I reacted by delivering a little lecture, which my wife did not receive well. We had words, and I went upstairs. A short while later, I apologized ungraciously. The apology was accepted, but not reciprocated.

That, for me least, was the lance that pierced the boil. I had condescended to show some remorse for something that I truly believed wasn't really my fault. How *dare* she not apologize in return? I said nothing at the time, but the demon was out. I smouldered with resentment for the rest of the day. I felt depressed, heavy and irritable about everything. Life suddenly became bitter and grey — and all over an item out of place!

This is resentment: the conscious act of nursing a grudge against a fellow human being for a real or imagined wrong they have committed against us. Someone fails to live up to our expectations, gets in our way, interrupts our plans, won't follow our agenda or meet our deadlines. And when we correct, these persons compound their wrongs by refusing to straighten up and fly right. They may, if they are very accommodating, try to toe the line for a while, but inevitably they fail to become the people we would like them to be.

The result: we resent them. We sulk. We brood. We analyze them endlessly and fruitlessly. We work ourselves up and get frustrated. And all our frustration, our failure to correct the other person's supposed wrongs lead us to become more angry, more resentful and more miserable within ourselves. Meanwhile the object of our resentment goes on with their life. They may recover from the spat and even interact with us as if it never happened. They begin to act as if this really wasn't the end of the world...

How dare they!

Spiritually speaking, resentment is our reaction to discovering that we cannot control the personalities and actions of others. In short, we are not God. When people around us fail to submit and act on cue, according to our directions, the limits of our power over them is exposed and we lash out like a thwarted petty tyrant throwing a tantrum. As this "inner Napoleon," kicks and screams, he may hurt others, but his ultimate victim is the soul that he inhabits, namely, our own. That's why resentment so often leaves us feeling far worse than the person against whom our resentment is directed. As someone once said, "Resentment is the poison we drink, hoping someone else will die."

Petty and imagined grievances notwithstanding, people often act in ways that really cross our boundaries, offend, injure or even abuse us. When such actions reveal our lack of godlike power, however, we are the ones who decide to react by throwing the inner paroxysm that wreaks so much spiritual and emotional havoc in our hearts and minds. Suffering is a reality for any created being. Because we are limited, we are subject to the forces beyond our control. However, resentment of our suffering is a choice we make, the futile fist-shaking of one who would be God and won't accept his humanity.

If resentment is a spiritual ailment, rooted in the failure of our godlike ambitions, then the cure must also be spiritual. I am not talking merely about more religious activity: prayer, Bible reading, church attendance — good and beneficial as these are. I am talking about concrete action. When others do things to expose our human limitations, we must face the revelation without seeking to escape from them through fantasy, analysis, entertainment, spending, etc. Next we must surrender our struggles to a Power greater than oneself: not just God in the abstract, but God as He makes Himself known in people who are objective, who love us, and who are not afraid to tell us the truth about ourselves. Only then can the abscess of our prideful egos be lanced and drained, and true healing begin.

The end result of this healing is the exact opposite of resentment: acceptance. God is God, and I am simply a member of the human race. To quote from page 449 of the Big Book of Alcoholics Anonymous: "Acceptance is the answer to all my problems today. When I am disturbed, it is because I find some person, place, thing or situation—some fact of my life—unacceptable to me, and I can find no serenity until I accept that person, place, thing or situation as being exactly the way it is supposed to be at this moment. Nothing, absolutely nothing happens in God's world by mistake... Unless I accept life completely on life's terms, I cannot be happy. I need to concentrate not so much on what needs to be changed in the world as on what needs to be changed in me and in my attitudes."

May 2009

Scapegoating

You may wonder where the term "scapegoat" comes from. As a matter of fact, it comes from the Book of Leviticus:

"Aaron shall lay both his hands upon the head of the live goat, and confess over him all the iniquities of the people of Israel, and all their transgressions, all their sins; and he shall put them upon the head of the goat, and send him away into the wilderness by the hand of a man who is in readiness. The goat shall bear all their iniquities upon him to a solitary land; and he shall let the goat go in the wilderness." (Lev. 16:21-22)

A scapegoat, therefore, referred literally to an 'escaped goat' in the wilderness. It was necessary because the people of Israel could not enter into any kind of relationship with God unless that which separated them from Him—sins and transgressions—were 'sent away.' Unlike the burnt offerings, which served as a way of repairing a person's failure to keep the covenant with God, the purpose of the scapegoat was to psychologically and spiritually send the nation's collective guilt back to the realm from which it came—the wilderness, which was understood in Scripture as the home of demons.

The prescriptions of Leviticus for Israel are a communal, symbolic form of what you and I often do on a daily basis. I am talking about scapegoating (my spell check tells me it doesn't exist, but I beg to differ). When we do something wrong, we often cannot stand to bear the blame alone. Our guilt is more than we can endure. We need to put some distance between it and ourselves somehow...

That's where scapegoating comes in. By placing our sins and transgressions 'upon the head' of someone or something else, send it away from ourselves, perhaps we can be free from the shame that we cannot bear.

How does scapegoating work? Consider those subtle non-apologies we are so good at. "I'm sorry I snapped at you. I've just been so stressed lately... I'm sorry I'm late. The kids were really dragging their feet this morning."

It's rarely just, "I'm sorry I snapped. There's no excuse," or something equally responsible. We 'admit' the guilt, then quickly transfer it—often in the same breath. External circumstances (such as stress) and other people (such as the kids) become our scapegoats. We have even mastered the trick of making our own psychological states (depression, medical illness, inherited conditions) the causes of our negative actions, rather than what they really are: the conditions that incline us to act in certain ways, but do not cause them.

For instance, the chronic pain I feel as a result of some ailment is not the cause of my irritability. My pain may make me more susceptible to anger, but nothing and no one can actually *make* me angry. The temptations to act in certain ways may come from specific external sources, but the acts themselves are my full responsibility.

But that's just the problem. Most of the time, we seem unable bear this responsibility. We need a scapegoat, and by hook or crook, we often find one, for a time at least. Eventually, when we commit more or different wrongs, we need new scapegoats, and the process of blame transference begins all over again.

Like all sinful tendencies in the human soul, scapegoating is a natural instinct used for unnatural purposes. The truth is, we *can't* really bear our own wrongful behaviours; left to fester, they *will* destroy us. Unless we find someone else to bear our shame and guilt, our shame and guilt will begin to poison us.

We need a scapegoat, but it can't be other people: friends, family, coworkers. It can't be circumstances or conditions in which we find ourselves. Those are temporary fixes at best, and in the end they really don't work. Inevitably, scapegoating disconnects us from ourselves and the world around us, leading to alienation, isolation and spiritual death.

Who or what, then, can be our scapegoat? According to an

Eastern Orthodox reading of the Old Testament Scriptures, the prescriptions of Leviticus are not merely social, psychological or even religious techniques for dealing with guilt. They are rather *prophecies* fulfilled in the Person of Jesus Christ. Christ Himself is the ultimate scapegoat who "bore our sins" (1 Peter 2:24) in the wilderness "outside the camp" (Hebrews 13:13).

Being fully human, Jesus understands human weakness, and so can identify with the burdens that we give Him. Being fully God, though, He can really and truly and completely take away the sins we give Him. With Christ, we are not simply emptying our trash into someone else's yard. We are sending it into eternity and oblivion.

In this view, God is not just a God to whom we can turn over our will and our lives, so that He might provide for our emotional, spiritual and material needs. He is the God to whom we can turn over our wrongs as well! And when the conditions that led us into wrongdoing come upon us, we can say, "I don't want to bear this; I want You to bear it for me; I put it upon Your head." It's inconceivable that our inconceivably loving God could make this provision for us, but it's true. We don't need to figure it out. All we need to do is accept it.

July 2009

The Anatomy of Fear

Chapter 3 of the Book of Genesis illustrates a telling moment in the spiritual history of the human race. Adam and Eve have disobeyed God's commandment and eaten the fruit of the knowledge of good and evil. By doing so, they have effectively declared themselves to "like God," (Gen. 3:5) which is to say, His equals.

In that moment, Adam and Eve discover that they are in fact naked: "Then the eyes of both were opened, and they knew that they were naked; and they sewed fig leaves together and made themselves aprons." (Gen. 3:7)

The nakedness of Adam and Eve is more than just physical nudity. It also represents their spiritual intimacy with each other, the world, and ultimately, God Himself. Nakedness means they are open, transparent, and vulnerable. Nothing is hidden, nothing concealed. They are fully exposed to and therefore known by God.

By discovering their nakedness and sewing fig leaves into aprons, our spiritual ancestors demonstrate that they can no longer live in this exposed state. As God's would-be equals they cannot allow Him to have direct access their souls. As rivals for His godhood, they must separate themselves from Him and define themselves against Him.

Of course, there is a problem: they are not the real God and never will be. And when the real God shows up, their first instinct is to avoid Him:

"And they heard the sound of the LORD God walking in the garden in the cool of the day, and the man and his wife hid themselves from the presence of the LORD God among the trees of the garden. But the LORD God called to the man, and said to him, "Where are you?" And he said, "I heard the sound of You in the garden, and I was afraid, because I was naked; and I hid myself."" (Gen. 3:8-10)

We are witnessing here the anatomy of fear. Adam and Eve's

claim to be God's equals lead them to separate themselves from Him by covering themselves up. They realize that their claim to godhood is false, but they are not willing to repent of it, so they would rather run away from the real God, in the forlorn hope that they can continue nurturing the illusion that they are "like God, knowing good and evil." (Gen 3:5)

What then is fear? It is simply the refusal to look at ourselves honestly, to take responsibility for who we really are. We persist in believing that we are the masters of our own destinies, even as we realize that we are living a lie. Fear is the attitude of running and hiding from the truth that we are not God.

All our fears have this common spiritual root. Consider, for instance, fear of economic insecurity — a common one these days. If I am constantly worried about my family's material wellbeing, is it not because I refuse to accept that I am not ultimately in control of the larger economic forces of the world? Isn't my fear just a stubborn insistence that I am playing god in my life, in spite of all evidence that it's just a game?

If this is indeed so, then the antidote to fear is two-fold. First, it is a courageous confrontation with the truth. We need to look squarely at the ways in which self-reliance has failed us, the ways in which we are really not "like God," the ways in which we are really powerless over our emotional, psychological, and material lives.

Secondly, the antidote to fear is a life lived in trust. We must stop running, turn and surrender ourselves to the real God. If there is any fear in our life at all, the chances are we worshiping the wrong God — an angry and judging and punishing and vengeful deity, an idol who keeps keep us running, enslaved to our fear.

And if we want to be free from fear, perhaps we should consider the possibility that another God might in fact exist, a God who wants to embrace us and care for us and who provide everything we need to live and thrive as His children.

The good news is that we do not need to believe

wholeheartedly in such a God. We need only acknowledge the possibility that <u>might</u> He be real. That acknowledgement is alone enough to open the door through which His love can flood in upon us, casting out all fear and filling us with our lives with real and lasting joy.

June 2010

The Final Frontier

"Space: the final frontier. These are the voyages of the star ship Enterprise. Her five-year mission: to explore strange new worlds, to seek out new life and new civilizations, to boldly go where no man has gone before."

The opening monologue from the original *Star Trek* television series expresses a fundamental impulse in the human spirit: the need to explore, to open up new frontiers, to discover new realities and experiences.

Our minds and hearts follow Neil Armstrong to the moon, Ferdinand Magellan around the world, Christopher Columbus onto the shores of the Americas, and Sir Edmund Hillary to the peak of Mount Everest. And as if that were not enough, we imagine Bilbo and Frodo Baggins crossing Middle Earth to fight dragons and destroy an evil Ring, young heroes and heroines questing for Aslan in the land of Narnia, Odysseus returning home to reunite with his wife and bring order to his household.

We long for accounts of adventures to realms unknown, where dangers abound and death is imminent, where a heart courageous and true might save the world, or least, find a great treasure and rescue a captive princess…

For most of us, though, the opportunities to "boldly go where no man has gone before" are somewhat limited. Most of us live in relative safety and comfort, with little effort required to stay fed, sheltered, and healthy. Few of us feel as if we have to accomplish some great task on which the survival of our world depends. This, in my opinion, is why we live these stories vicariously through movies and fantasy novels, or hang breathlessly on the most recent real life attempts to rescue trapped miners in Chile…

And yet the need to pioneer, explore, and adventure continues to cry out within us, even as we resign ourselves to a 21st century existence whose only excitement seems to be found on the screen of a television or a computer. A part of us knows this can't be all there is. There must be a real "final frontier" somewhere out there...

That's the problem, though. The answer to our deepest need to explore and pioneer does not lie "out there"—in ever wilder fantasies of literature and film, or ever more extreme and dangerous "real life" crises and disasters. Our questing spirits cannot be satisfied by escaping into other people's experiences or creations. Satisfaction must be found not "out there," but "in here," by which I mean in each and every human heart.

For twenty centuries, teachers of classical Christianity have understood the heart to be the centre of the spiritual life. In this, they were not thinking of the heart as representing the kinds of emotions depicted on greeting cards and carved on tree trunks. Rather, the early Fathers believed that the heart is the meeting place of the intellect and the bodily senses. One writer, Chariton, put it this way: "The heart is the innermost man or spirit. Here are located self-awareness, the conscience, the idea of God and one's complete dependence on Him, and all the eternal treasures of the spiritual life."

Nor were these teachers speaking of the heart as a mere symbol. As Theophan the Recluse says, "Prayer of the heart is not only prayer of the soul and spirit but also of the *body*. It must not be forgotten that the heart signifies, among other things, a bodily organ. The body has a positive role to play in the work of prayer."

The heart, then, is not just an idea or a symbol; it is a real place where the work of the spiritual life takes place. Indeed, the quintessential Eastern Orthodox way of prayer known as "the Way of Inner Stillness" begins by asking us to sit, close our eyes, lower our heads, and then to pray with all our attention in our physicals hearts.

What has this got to do with the human need to explore the frontiers of our world? An Egyptian hermit called Macarius offers an answer: "Within the heart are unfathomable depths. It is but a small vessel and yet dragons and lions are there, and there poisonous creatures and all the treasures of wickedness; rough, uneven paths are there, and gaping chasms. There likewise is God, there are the angels, there life and the Kingdom, there light and the Apostles, the heavenly cities and the treasures of grace; all things are there."

In short, I disagree with the writers of *Star Trek*: space is not the final frontier. Nothing "out there" is the final frontier. Only the heart is the final frontier. Only here can we find the one place where "no man has gone before" except us.

We spend hours journeying with others through the virtual and imaginary realms. Now is the time for a real adventure. Now is the time for a quest that is truly our own, one that will outdo the dangers and rewards of most daring explorations of mountains, oceans, galaxies, or any world the imagination can create.

How can you embark on this journey? It's very simple and inexpensive. First, clear some time in your day; it doesn't need to be very much time — ten minutes is all you will ever need. Next, sit down in a secluded spot. Lower your head and focus your attention on the place of your heart. Finally, quietly and repeatedly call upon the Name of God, which in the Eastern Orthodox tradition is the Name of Jesus Christ.

And that's it. Your quest has begun. May you find the treasure, rescue the princess, kill the dragon, destroy the evil Ring, meet the Great Lion, and return home safely. God speed — the survival of your world depends on you.

October 2010

The Problem with "isms"

We inhabit a world of "isms." There's fundamentalism, which preaches black and white, and relativism, which preaches only grey. Pluralism tells us that differences don't matter, while sectarianism insists that difference is everything. Individualism asserts the good of the one, tribalism the good of many.

As you may have guessed, an ism is a worldview, a philosophy, an ideology, a set of beliefs. Seeing the ills of society and the world, someone with the best of intentions comes up with an ism to make it all better.

At first glance, the ism looks quite appealing, mostly because it offers an all-encompassing solution to a big mess. The ism basically says, "If only we could do such-and-such, everything would be better." If only certain laws could be changed, if only people could be educated well enough, if only everyone could just follow *these* principles, all would be well. Wars would cease. Hunger and poverty would be eradicated. People would be happy. Simple.

But that's exactly the problem with isms, the fatal flaw that makes them the curse of the human race and potential source of our self-destruction. You see, even the most sophisticated ism is just too simplistic.

I read recently, for example, that the World Trade Center contained an Islamic prayer room that was a regular place of prayer for numerous Muslim staff and visitors. The room was, of course, destroyed in the terrorist attacks of September 11th, along with some of those who worshipped in it.

The fact of this prayer room was lost on the attackers. They didn't see the realities of the people who worked and played and prayed in the World Trade Center. Instead, enslaved to their ism, they saw the whole building and those within it as nothing more than a giant symbol of American Capitalism.

That's the problem with isms. In their quest to make the world a better place, they end up oversimplifying it. And in oversimplifying, they dehumanize. They reduce the multifaceted richness of human life to mere abstractions, lifeless ideas in the grand scheme to fix the world.

How can we respond to this destructive impulse? I have often voiced my conviction that Christianity properly understood is not merely another set of beliefs, an ism built on morality, the idea of God and the afterlife. Rather, I would argue that Christianity is the end of religion, a radical, transformative reality in which a loving God and His Creation are reconciled and reunited.

At the heart of Christian "non-religion" is the Person of Jesus Christ. In this Jewish male, who walked in Palestine two thousand years ago, who possessed a unique appearance, personality, culture and language, who had a particular way of walking and talking — in *this* person, Christianity says we meet the eternal, inconceivable, unapproachable God, Maker of the galaxies and atoms.

This strange and radical proclamation has some very real implications. If a unique and complex human being was the heart of God's self-revelation to the world, then the solution to the suffering of society, and the problems of the world as a whole must take place on a personal, human level. In short, the antidote to isms is a loving and intimate relationship with others.

Rather than saying, "If only so-and-so could just learn to live according to these principles," our challenge is to meet and accept each person, exactly as they present themselves to us. Rather than expecting people to behave in certain ways because they come from a certain culture or adhere to certain beliefs, we must strive to understand them as whole persons, their language, their story, their struggles. Rather than demanding cooperation of others because we believe we are right and know best, we need to work slowly and painstakingly to build their trust through loving and selfless service, without expectation.

And if our conviction calls us to proclaim to others the

Gospel we have received, we need to avoid the temptation to cajole, bribe, manipulate or coerce them into sharing our faith. We must learn to step back and allow the God in whom we believe to draw others to Himself, in His own time and manner.

Since the early Middle Ages, western societies (and those eastern societies we have influenced by our thought) have been marked by a reforming spirit — an impulse to make the world better by applying certain ideals and principles, by enacting certain manifestos in the form of revolutions, or by staging social, political and religious revivals. We are easily tempted to adopt isms, with tragic and bloody consequences that are even now playing themselves out across the globe.

If the Gospel has anything to say to us now, it is this: reject the temptation of isms. Reject the theoretical solutions that appear easy and elegant. Stop trying to reform the world with our systems of thought, philosophies, ideologies, and even our religions. Instead, take the time to meet and love our neighbours — the unique and complex human persons we encounter day by day — in whom we can also meet, if we desire it, the God who came to meet us in a human being.

April 2011

The Encounter in the Wilderness

Have you ever felt as if you have lost something on which you most depend? Perhaps your health or your physical abilities have been compromised. Perhaps you have lost a job or financial security. Maybe you are disconnected from your spouse, friends or family. Or perhaps you just feel emotionally disconnected from God.

Regardless of what certain 'prosperity Gospel' preachers might tell you, there is nothing wrong with you. You aren't being punished for some unspecified crime. You are not suffering because you are 'unclean' in some way. God is not shunning you. You have not taken a wrong turn in your spiritual journey.

On the contrary, such debilitating experiences are not only par for the course in our spiritual journey, they are the very conditions in which we grow and deepen our knowledge of God. If you are feeling deprived materially, physically, emotionally, psychologically or spiritually, you stand in good company.

Consider, for instance, the people of Israel. According to the Old Testament Scriptures, God took Israel out of Egypt, where they were enslaved but relatively comfortable, and brought them into the wilderness, where they wandered for forty years with no established dwelling place, with nothing to eat or drink, other than what God miraculously provided for them. In addition to these material deprivations, they suffered illness and death, saw friends and family perish, and endured God's wrath at their faithlessness and disobedience.

In the Orthodox Christian interpretation, the Old Testament narratives are ultimately a prophecy of the Person of Jesus Christ. In a personal fulfilment of Israel's collective exile, Jesus is taken as an infant into Egypt. Later, he enters the desert, where he is tempted and fed by angels. His ministry begins and is mostly directed at those who live "beyond the Jordan" (Matthew 4:25 and elsewhere), which in scriptural geography symbolizes the wilderness from which Israel came before it entered the Promised Land. Finally, Jesus is crucified outside the walls of Jerusalem, which the New Testament writer to the Hebrews likens to the wilderness "outside the camp" of Israel. (Hebrews 13:11-14)

Jesus' experience of human life as a wilderness is crucial to the Christian confession that he "emptied himself, taking the form of a servant, being born in the likeness of men. And being found in human form he humbled himself and became obedient unto death, even death on a cross." (Phil. 2:7-8) Only in the condition of utter humility, utter emptiness, utter brokenness, stripped of all human power and aid, could God's power full shine forth in him. Only by being crucified as a criminal outside the camp could He be exalted on the third day and receive "the name which is above every name," the Son of God to whom all authority in heaven and on earth is given. (See Phil. 2:9 and Matt. 28:18)

What does this mean for us? Simply that, for Christians at least, the wilderness experience is central to our encounter with God. When we are stripped of dependence on human aid, whether that involves losing our physical health or material resources, or being deprived of emotional or psychological or spiritual convictions in our hearts and minds, we are embarking on nothing less important and significant than the journey to the Cross of Christ, where the power and glory of God shines forth most brightly.

Of course, knowing that being "united with him in a death like his, we shall certainly be united with him in a resurrection like his," (Romans 6:5) does not in any way alleviate the physical pain of an illness, the uncertainty of unemployment, or the agony of family division and conflict. Regardless of what we know to be true in our minds, when we find ourselves in the thick of our wilderness sufferings, we cannot help but cry out with the Psalmist, "O LORD, why do You cast me off? Why do You hide Your face from me?" (Psalm 88:14)

Faced with such circumstances, I have often recalled the

words of the poet T.S. Eliot: "I have lost sight, smell, hearing, taste and touch; how can I use them for your closer contact?" Notice to whom the poet addresses his question. In the wilderness, I am stripped of every support and help, *including my own ability to reason out and comprehend why this is happening to me*. My only option is to throw myself outward to a Power greater than myself, who alone can show forth the light in my darkness, the resurrection in my crucifixion. All I can do is ask *Him* the questions, and wait for *Him* to show the answers.

Those answers may be slow in coming (often they come only years in retrospect) and are often couched in unexpected and surprising terms. For this wanderer in the spiritual wilderness, however, they have always come in the end.

If you stand in the wilderness of your life today, devoid of all other earthly help, you stand on the front line of the spiritual battle, for you have come the place where you can truly encounter the One who will lead you "through the great and terrible wilderness, with its fiery serpents and scorpions and thirsty ground where there [is] no water… that he might humble you and test you, to do you good in the end." (Deut. 8:15-16)

August 2009

"You Are Not What You Do."

Up until a week ago, I was on vacation. During that time, in which I did little more than float on an inflatable mattress in the middle of a lake, I reflected on how our culture equates activity with identity. Quite simply, we *are* what we *do*.

As an Eastern Orthodox priest, I do many things. I am the husband of my wife and the father of my three small children. I am writer by profession and passion. Finally, I am a pastor by vocation, serving the many services on the Church calendar, calling and visiting my people, preparing sermons, studies and teachings, as well as praying daily and trying simply to be a good Christian. It's a full and busy life.

Do all these activities add up to *me*? Our culture would suggest that they do. Our various jobs, hobbies, vocations, roles define us. Without them, who are we? If I subtract husband, father, writer and pastor from my life, who is left? The world around me would tend to answer, "No one." On the other hand, when I am busy, doing all those tasks "successfully," then the world acknowledges that I am Someone. It may not necessarily like what I am doing, but at least I am a "contributing member of society."

Religion is often understood in these functional terms. If I go to church, give money, pray, do good deeds, then I am a "good" person in God's eyes. If I fail to do the above, then He does not value me as much. This ancient and conventional religiosity goes back to the days when a sacrifice was thought to appease the deity.

Christianity, however, offers a radical alternative to the equation of activity with identity. In the lectionary this past Sunday, we saw Jesus heal a paralytic who doesn't *do* or even *say* anything. (Matt. 9:1-8) He simply receives the healing, which is occasioned only by the loving faithfulness of those who carry him. Seeing the witness of his family and friends, Jesus offers the paralytic the forgiving embrace of God for all of broken human and refers to him as "my son," which is to say, a co-heir of God's kingdom. (see Gal. 4:7)

This encounter tells us emphatically that we are *not* what we do. If Jesus healed a man who did nothing to deserve it, then whether or not we are good spouses, parents, friends, or workers, has no bearing whatever on God's view of us. As parents, do we think: "I love my children now, but I will love them more when they have achieved a Bachelor's degree, written a book, or won the Nobel prize"? If we are even moderately functional, we simply love them, for no other reason than the fact that they exist! Of course, human parents often fall prey to the temptation of conditional love, but God never does. From the moment He created us, we have been good, beloved, precious and holy to Him. No amount of failure or betrayal can denigrate us, no amount of success can possibly exalt us in His eyes.

Of course, Jesus healed the paralytic because He saw the faith of that man's family. Which means that although *we* can do nothing to engender God's love, we do have the responsibility to bring God's eternal and divine love into our daily encounters with self and others. I engage with all the activities of my life in this world — husband, father, writer, priest — to the best of my ability, not to prove that I am a worthwhile person, but so that I and those around me may know the goodness and love of God. In the end, I am not worthwhile because of what I do. I am worthwhile because God made me and loves me. And everything else I do — for myself and for others — I do to remember that awe-inspiring fact every day.

July 2008

To the Unknown God

For Spiritual Seekers

Recently, I spoke with a group of students at the College of the Rockies about religion and culture. During the question time, one of the students asked how someone who is not attached to any particular church or religion or belief system, could learn about the spiritual life. In her own diplomatic way, she was asking me to provide her with a set of guidelines to discover the truth (or falsity) of my statements apart from the presuppositions of my Christian faith.

It was a tall order, and I don't think I did it justice in the time that I had. In the weeks since, however, I have had the opportunity to consider this important question further and to assemble a more coherent answer. I still cannot claim perfect objectivity, but then again, who can? What follows is one priest's effort to offer guidance to spiritual seekers beyond the borders of Christianity.

Before taking the first step in the journey to discover spiritual reality, we must take what might be called, Step "Zero," and *commit to an attitude of rigorous honesty*. If there is a real spiritual dimension beyond ourselves, it must also exist beyond our power to create, control or manipulate. In other words, we can't make up spiritual reality as we go along, according to our whims and imaginations; if it exists, it must exist objectively, that is, *whether we like it or not*.

If we are going to embark on the journey into the realm of the spirit, then, we must first accept that we may discover some difficult truths, demands, challenges, and even refutations, all of which we may have to both face and accept. If our exploration is going to be truly fruitful, therefore (as opposed to a mere fabrication of our intellect and imagination), we must resolve from the beginning to be ruthlessly honest. If the spiritual life exists, we will embrace it wholeheartedly in whatever form it takes, without seeking to deny or avoid its rigors and sufferings.

This alone is not an easy step to take, but without taking it, we cannot hope to discover anything resembling a reality outside of ourselves. Having made this first commitment, though, we can take the actual first step on the spiritual journey and *begin a conversation with the divine.*

Is there a God? Does this God love or care for us personally, or is "It" just an impersonal, indifferent or malignant force? Unfortunately, scientific reasoning cannot help us here, because the very definition of God's identity precludes our ability to encompass "It" with our intellects. As soon as I am able to define God within parameters that I myself have determined, then God is no longer God—a transcendent power beyond me. Rather, I am holding the strings, which makes *me* God.

In other words, we can't get "behind" God in order to prove God's existence. The only way to discover the reality or truth of some universal Higher Power (or whatever you choose to call it) is for us simply to initiate a conversation. Say something like this: "If you exist, I am ready and willing to accept you, whoever or whatever you are. If you exist, reveal yourself to me as you really are." Repeat these words every day for three months, and (in the spirit of Step "Zero") be ready to accept *whatever* may result from the effort, whether you like the answer or not.

Given that some kind of response to your prayer is forthcoming, the next step in the process is to *find a communal root* for your spiritual life. As human beings, we do not live well in abstraction and isolation. For whatever reason, we need to ground our lives in other people. As I have heard it said, "There is no me without you." And Jean Vanier, the founder of L'Arche, has said that our need to belong is more fundamental than our need to be loved! For mysterious reasons, individuals need to live in community. Anything less seems to be a recipe for self-destruction...

What is true of the four-dimensional life is also true of a life that integrates within it the spiritual dimension. "God" is an abstract concept, and one that lives mostly in our intellects unless we root it in a concrete expression outside of ourselves: a community to which we are accountable. If we really believe in a power greater than ourselves, a reality that governs our existence, then that power and reality must take this tangible, communal form outside of "me, myself and I."

I would therefore suggest that as you begin the spiritual journey, you find a community with which you can "travel." Look for a group of healthy-minded individuals who care for one another and those around them. Look for sound leaders who care more for their people than themselves. Look for freedom, joy, peace, lack of judgment, but also honesty and steadfastness of belief.

Whatever community you find, be sure that they are willing to call you to account, to challenge you and even if necessary to rebuke you if you wander off the path to which you have committed. Again, this goes back to Step "Zero"; the community guarantees that we will not avoid those aspects of the spiritual reality that are personally unpleasant or inconvenient.

The third and final step is to *put your house in order*. There are many "spiritual" people who in fact use their spirituality as a prop to shore up their personal dependencies, addictions, and neuroses. Religion can easily become a "substitute addiction" for a person who struggles with these compulsive behaviors. The problem lies at the heart of the individual, who (usually due to childhood abuse) feels utterly powerless of his or her life and therefore will use anything — drugs, alcohol, food, relationships, money, work, and religion — to maintain the illusion of control.

As you embark on the spiritual life, therefore, it is essential that you also discover if traces of addiction or compulsion lie within you, waiting to poison your best spiritual intentions. The best way to root out potential problems is to seek a course of counseling with a professional who respects the spiritual dimension of human existence and who has a reputation for honesty and tough love. You needn't commit to a lifetime of counseling, but a three month course can go a long way to exposing the emotional and psychological "hand of cards" that life has dealt you.

If, during in this period of time, you discover that you have specific addiction and/or dependency, begin to address it through a program of recovery that respects the life of the spirit. In my opinion, 12-Step programs are the most helpful in this regard. And in case you may be thinking that "12-Step" refers only to alcoholism, you should know that there is a 12-Step program for every major addiction, from food (Overeaters Anonymous) and drugs (Narcotics Anonymous), to gambling (Gambler's Anonymous) and sexual addictions (Sexaholics Anonymous).

To review, then, the steps to beginning the spiritual life are as follows:

Commit to an attitude of rigorous honesty.
Begin a conversation with the divine.
Find a communal root.
Put your house in order.

Where these spiritual steps will lead, I will not say. One thing is certain, however: if you follow them, *something* will happen, something profound and life-changing, painful and joyful. Reality will open up, and once it does, there's no going back. Before you proceed, therefore, take heed to the warnings of ancient cartographers: *beyond here there be dragons*. More than that, though, there be new worlds and unimaginably wide horizons. May God speed you on the voyage.

February 2010

209

Daily Spiritual Renewals

A number of years ago, someone approached a minister friend of mine and told him that she was an agnostic seeking spiritual enlightenment. To his credit, my friend did not preach at her or offer her a trite "solution" to her quandary. Instead, he simply said, "Good. Keeping searching. Just remember: no B.S."

The AA 12 Step program, which considers itself both non-sectarian and non-religious, tells us that a "No B.S." policy of rigorous honesty is crucial to healing the spiritual ailment at the root of alcoholism. The same holds true, I believe, to every psychologically or emotionally wounded human being on the planet. No matter where you come from, no matter what your belief, honesty is the foundation for progress in the spiritual life.

Honesty is the act of telling the truth about ourselves. It is looking at ourselves squarely in the physical, psychological, emotional and spiritual mirror, and being willing to face *whatever* we see there, no matter how painful it may be. It is to acknowledge where we stand and who we are right now, without resorting to denial or escape.

According to AA and other spiritual traditions, the first conclusion to which honesty leads us is that we cannot go it alone. We need a Higher Power outside and beyond ourselves to find healing and self-fulfilment. This Higher Power can take different forms. For some atheist or agnostic alcoholics, for example, a local AA home group is the Higher Power in which they trust. However it is expressed, though, the Higher Power must possess one crucial quality: a loving nature. The "God of our understanding" has to be seeking our ultimate wellbeing, and not our harm or destruction.

Having realized our inability to fix ourselves, and our need for a loving Higher Power (Steps One, Two and Three of the 12-Step program), we have effectively begun the spiritual life. To make progress and grow, however, we must regularly examine ourselves and rededicate our commitment to the Higher Power who will heal us and bring us closer to our true and fulfilled identities.

In this process, experience has shown that we need not only the Higher Power, but also other human beings. Why? Because restricting our self-examination to our own minds and hearts can lead to self-deception and more denial. As one AA friend of mine put it: "My mind is dangerous neighbourhood. I never go there alone."

Spiritual renewal, then, means making a "fearless moral inventory" (Step 4 of the 12-Step program) and then sharing that inventory, both with our Higher Power *and another human being*. When we make a declaration before a witness, the spiritual rubber hits the road, and we can really be sure that honesty — and therefore healing — is really and concretely at work in us. Honesty in our minds is merely theoretical. Honesty offered out loud to someone else is *incarnate*, and therefore *real* in a way that it can never be in the abstractions of our private thoughts.

Real spiritual progress flows from regular spiritual renewals of the above kind — daily, if possible. As long as "No B.S." is the motto, a renewal can take many forms, and may be undertaken with any person that we trust and love, as long as they are genuinely seeking our wellbeing. To that end, if we are involved in an addiction of any sort (alcohol, drugs, sex, anger, gambling, co-dependency, etc.), we may not want to do a daily renewal with someone who enables our addictive behaviour...

With those guidelines in mind, I would like to share with you a daily spiritual renewal that I have undertaken with my wife, usually after the kids are asleep and we are in bed (squabbles and complaints tend to detract from our spiritual focus). As the 12-Step saying goes, "Take what you want and leave the rest." And may the Higher Power of God grant you a renewed spiritual life, wherever you may be!

January 2009

A Daily Spiritual Renewal

Guidelines for sharing:
Nothing is too great or small to be shared.
Let there be no criticism or judgement of others
Let there be no advice-giving, unless requested.
Everything shared should be kept confidential.

Begin by saying the "Serenity Prayer" together:
"God, grant me the serenity to accept the things I cannot change, courage to change the things I can, and wisdom to know the difference. Your will, not mine, be done."

Each person takes turns to share, answering the following:
7. **In the past 24 hours**, I have struggled with fear or worry about _____.
8. **In the past 24 hours**, I have struggled with anger or resentment about _____.
9. **In the past 24 hours**, I have been grateful for _____.
10. **In the past 24 hours**, I sought the Presence of God by __ __.

11. **For the next 24 hours**, what will I *specifically* do to maintain my spiritual health? (Examples: spiritual reading, reaching out and calling others, prayer and meditation, going to Church, caring for my body, setting proper boundaries)
12. **For the next 24 hours**, what situations or personal encounters could threaten my spiritual health? How can I avoid them or deal with them appropriately?
13. **Right now**, am I *truly* willing to surrender my will and my life to the care of God for the next 24 hours?

End by repeating the "Serenity Prayer"

The God-Shaped Hole

See if you can identify with the following scene. It's Christmas morning, and everyone is gathered around the tree. Presents are handed out and the sound of tearing wrappers fills the air. At first the children squeal with excitement as they discover the gifts. It's a Kodak moment, the picture perfect Christmas.

Then, slowly, the atmosphere shifts. With their presents unwrapped and laid out before them, the children start to squabble amongst themselves. If you have very little ones, like I do, they seem to become overwhelmed by the sheer mass of stuff they now possess. They become more selfish, demanding and peevish, or else withdraw to play with the wrappers and the boxes rather than the presents themselves. They are easily provoked to tears. Adults, a little more nuanced in their behavior, stack their collection of gifts carefully in a corner, and try to ignore the faint but distinct hollowness within.

That's it. Christmas is over. We purchased our stuff in a frenzy of feverish activity, then wrapped carefully and placed them beneath the tree. But now, with wrappings strewn around like the victims of tornado, the stuff is, well, just more stuff to be added to the rest of the stuff we already possess.

Somehow it never quite ends as it was supposed to, as we hope it will, Christmas after Christmas. Our children, so excited by the potential of unwrapping their gifts, seem unhappier after the fact than before it. More possessions, rather than satisfying, seem to have made us less content than they were before.

This is the paradoxical tragedy of materialism. The more we own, the happier we're supposed to be. The reality is, though, the more we have, the more ungrateful, dissatisfied, peevish, demanding, or simply indifferent, we become. We want to fill some hole within ourselves, and we are duped year after year into thinking that the appropriate filler is a new Xbox or the latest installment of *Toy Story*. But these and other material things, rather than filling the hole inside us, seem to expand it instead.

In Jesus' parable of the banquet from the Gospel of Saint Luke, we hear of a man "who gave a great banquet, and invited many. At the time for the banquet he sent his servant to say to those who had been invited, 'Come; for all is now ready.' But they all alike began to make excuses. The first said to him, 'I have bought a field, and I must go out and see it; I pray you, have me excused." And another said, 'I have bought five yoke of oxen, and I go to examine them; I pray you, have me excused.' And another said, 'I have married a wife, and therefore I cannot come.'" (Luke 14:16-20)

Why do the invited guests refuse the invitation? Simply because they have a bunch of stuff, on which they are completely focused, to the exclusion of all else. They are possessed by the desire to fulfill all the basic human needs: the need to belong and have a place (symbolized by the field); the need for physical survival by consuming food and drink (symbolized by the yoke of oxen); and the need for relationship and community (symbolized by the marriage).

However, the fulfillment of these material needs has made the potential guests both ungrateful and totally unresponsive to the generosity of the householder. The joy of the feast, which in other Gospels is actually a marriage feast that a king holds for his son, is lost on them because they believe they have already filled the hole of their needs. That's why the lord of the household sends his servants to bring the poor, the maimed, the blind and the lame to share in the banquet. (Luke 14:21) They have nothing. They are hungry and needy and so their response to the invitation will be wholehearted and joyful.

I heard it said once that every human being has a "God-shaped hole" within them—an emptiness, a yearning for something more, something bigger than they are. Every year, we turn Christmas into a season when we frantically try to fill that hole with something—presents, good cheer, family, and even a little religion—in the hope that perhaps this time, the hole will be diminished just a little, if not filled in completely.

The climactic moment on Christmas morning—when the season explodes like a cracker with the cheap toys and paper crowns inside, and all we are left with is a pile of stuff and an emptiness even greater than before—that moment is a reminder that the God-shaped hole cannot be filled in the way we have been led to believe. The field, the five yoke of oxen and the wife—all the stuff we have in our life—just won't cut it, because they are the wrong shape and ultimately, too small for the size of the hole we want to fill.

In the end, only the infinite God can fill the God-shaped hole. Our natural hunger for the divine, which savvy marketers cunningly manipulate to drive us into the malls, can be filled by none other than Him. Perhaps this Christmas, we will take that truth to heart and accept the invitation to the one feast that will truly satisfy us: the feast of the One who is the bread of life, the fattened calf, the wine that gladdens our hearts forever.

December 2010

God Without Church?

It's a common reality: people who believe in God without feeling the need to attend church regularly. They even have a name — "Nones" — because of their typical response to surveys asking about their religious affiliation. And those of us who consider Church attendance to be central to our faith might want ask ourselves why they are one of the most rapidly-growing demographics in North America.

What leads a person to believe in God, while refusing to identify themselves as members of a particular "faith community"?

These days, the answer would seem self-evident. Consider the genocides, the acts of terrorism, racism, and oppression by those who proudly claim to represent Christianity, Islam, Judaism and Hinduism. Witness the petty infighting, sectarianism, power-mongering, and divisiveness within religious communities. Add to this the various abuses inflicted by religious authorities on their weakest members, and it's not difficult to understand why someone might want to have nothing to do with a church at all.

As a pastor who must deal daily with some of this religious madness in my own Eastern Orthodox Church, I can genuinely understand the impulse to withdraw from the trials and tribulations of the spiritual life in community, and to seek out what people have frequently referred to as a "personal faith."

It is tempting to assemble our own set of beliefs about God, picking and choosing those elements that we find the most comforting, beautiful or simple. It is tempting to establish our own routine of prayer and meditation, our own spiritually meaningful rituals. It is tempting to want to be free from commitment to a church community, especially when such commitment often seems more draining than uplifting...

Why not take this path? Wouldn't it just be so much easier to believe without all that formal, institutional stuff that just seems to make a mess of things?

The heart of the answer lies in the definition of the word "believe." After all, what does it mean to believe in something, anyway? For many "Nones," spiritual belief implies an intellectual acceptance of certain ideas about God. It makes logical sense that there is some Higher Power, an ordering Force behind everything. It makes logical sense to speak of right and wrong, good and bad. And it makes logical sense that we should pay attention in some way to something beyond our material lives.

If we look closer, though, this kind of belief has nothing really to do with the actual existence of God. Rather, it's really all about me and my needs, and if a belief in God or some Higher Power helps me with those needs, so much the better. I can pick or discard the tenets of my belief system, as I need them. I can take or leave a faith community, depending on whether or not it meets my needs. I can even stop believing, if that helps. Because, ultimately, God is not the point here—the *idea* of God is the point, and then only in as much as it helps me fulfil my individual potential as a productive, healthy, well-rounded, well-adjusted, friendly, and more tolerant citizen of society and the world.

There is, however, another definition of what it means to believe. The original Hebrew and Greek words for "belief" are the same as "faith," and they imply an active spirit of faithfulness, trust, and support.

Belief in the scriptural sense is a choice to enter into a living relationship with divine reality. We don't just acknowledge the logic of God's existence because it's helpful to do so. We *commit* ourselves to His existence, which means submitting to Him in faithfulness and accountability and most importantly, sacrificing our personal inclinations, whims, and desires, to His higher power and will.

But can't we still have a "personal faith" without committing to membership in a Church community? Because values like accountability, sacrifice, commitment and trust are mere abstractions unless they involve other people. And unless we are willing to submit our beliefs for others to challenge, correct or even reject, our faith will remain locked inside our heads, a set of self-created ideas detached from reality.

The point of living in a community united by one faith is precisely to make our experience of God real by working it out in relation with human beings who are walking the same path as ours. Without these relationships — what I would call "communion" — we cannot meaningfully believe in God because we cannot commit to, submit to, sacrifice to, trust, or love a Power greater than ourselves in a real, tangible way.

So, if an intellectual belief in the idea of God is what we want, Church may not be for us. It may prove destructive to our most cherished notions. It may challenge us, make us uncomfortable, or force us to answer questions we would rather avoid.

If, however, a real belief in an actual God is what we want, we must be ready to meet Him in the only way possible: by engaging in human relationships, as messy, frustrating, crazy-making, and heart-breaking as they can be. Only by participating in Church life, with all the pains and sorrows of commitment, responsibility, accountability and sacrifice, can we ultimately reach the true end of our spiritual journey: peace and joy in union with each other and with the One who made us to love and be loved by Him for eternity.

December 2010

Panentheism

In his seminal work of theology, *For the Life of the* World, the Eastern Orthodox theologian Fr. Alexander Schmemann made a bold claim. He asserted that contrary to popular opinion, Christianity is not actually a religion at all. "Religion," he says, "is needed where there is a wall of separation between God and man. But Christ who is both God and man has broken down the wall between God and man. He has inaugurated a new life, not a new religion."

But isn't Christianity one of the world's 'great religions,' alongside Islam, Judaism, Buddhism and Hinduism? Can't Christianity be described as a 'faith system,' with tenets, rules and rituals, just like every other religion?

Yes and no. It is certainly true that Christianity resembles a religion. It has scriptures and spiritual writings, patterns of communal worship, methods of prayer and meditation. Some of us have formal sacramental rituals, such as Baptism and the Eucharist. Our beliefs can be described in creeds and catecheses. In short, Christianity *appears* very religious upon first inspection.

A closer look, however, reveals that while Christianity is superficially religious, its inward reality is very distinct from traditional notions of religion, which tend to fall into two distinct categories. First are what may be called *pantheistic* religions, which equate the cosmos with the divine principle. All natural things may thus be worshipped as gods, since all of them (the sun, the moon, the earth, the trees and rivers, and any animal) are simply frequencies of the same divine radiance.

Although pantheism says that one may encounter specific and concrete aspects of God, the divinity itself—sometimes described as the sum total of all that ever was, is, and ever shall be—remains abstract and unattainable. In that sense, pantheistic faiths *are* religions: systems of beliefs and ritualistic mechanisms that mediate between humanity and an unknowable divinity.

The second category of religion might be called *theism*. In contrast to pantheism, theism asserts the idea of a transcendent Divinity who exists above and beyond the cosmos. But while God is wholly other from the world that He created, most theistic faiths teach that God has established laws, moral codes, scriptures, and even rituals as points of mediation between God and His creation.

While many Christians might call themselves theists, I would suggest that theism itself is not a full and authentic expression of Christianity. While we can know *about* God through a text (such as the Bible or the Koran) or a sacrament (such as the Eucharist or the *Seder*), we can't actually encounter the Person of God Himself. Like a restricted form of pantheism, the theist God is still mediated by things, and as such the religious 'wall of separation' remains standing.

Radically, Christianity offers a third alternative to religion in its pantheist and theist varieties. The classic teaching of Christianity begins theistically: there is one, all-powerful, transcendent God who says of Himself, "As the heavens are higher than the earth, so are my ways higher than your ways and my thoughts than your thoughts." (Isaiah 55:9) According to Christianity, however, this transcendent God, who is above all things, mystically united Himself to His creation in and through the flesh of His Son Jesus Christ.

And the most profound mystery of all is that in becoming a man, God did not get lost in His creation. Just as Christ's human and divine natures were never confused and mingled, so too God remains distinct from His creation, still the one God, YHWH, who revealed Himself to Abraham, Isaac, Jacob and Moses. Christianity is neither pantheist (equating God with the cosmos), nor theist (separating God from the cosmos). Rather, God's Incarnation in Jesus Christ lifted up the cosmos, binding it forever to His divine nature, so that the universe itself becomes the full revelation of the one Godhead that always transcends the universe.

This is what might be called the 'panentheist' vision of Christianity. Panentheism, which means literally 'all in God' neither seeks to worship the things of this world (pantheism), nor seeking revelation and illumination in specific religious activities (theism). Rather, for the panentheist, the transcendent Presence of God lies at the heart of the ordinary activities of our lives — work and play and family — like a great bonfire waiting to purify and transform us with its flame. The things of this world are not fragmentary sources of the divine, but channels for the divine fountainhead which flows 'from above' and is not of this world. (John 8:23) Divine grace is not mediated only in specific texts or sacramental rituals; rather, life *itself* is a sacrament. Simply by living our lives as genuine human beings, we can actually meet God and know Him, not just intellectually, but intimately, actually, and completely.

So if Christianity is the end of all religion, why do we need its formal religious aspects at all? Why go to Church, read the Bible, pray, get baptized, or partake in the Eucharist? A little analogy to conclude. As a parent, I am always teaching my children how to say "thank you" with the intention of instilling in them a spirit of gratitude for the gift of life. Without this attitude, the words "thank you" are mere politeness at best, and cynicism and superficiality at worst. But having the attitude without the form is equally meaningless. After all, abstract gratitude without an *expression* of gratitude has just as little force as an insincere "thank you."

So it is with Christianity. Unless we live as panentheists, immersing our whole life in God, our Christianity is nothing more than dead, nominal religion. But equally necessary are Christianity's texts, spiritual traditions and sacramental rituals, by which we fulfill our 'all in God' way of life by naming the Source of that way in our Lord Jesus Christ, who is proclaimed and handed down from the beginning, who made His divine life human to make our human life divine.

April 2009